Dánta Ban

POEMS OF IRISH WOMEN
EARLY AND MODERN

Selected and Translated
by

P. L. Henry D. Phil., D. Litt., M.R.I.A.

THE MERCIER PRESS

The Mercier Press, 4 Bridge Street, Cork
24 Lower Abbey Street, Dublin 1

© P. L. Henry, 1990
First published 1991

British Library Cataloguing in Publication Data
Dánta Ban: poems of Irish women early and modern
  1. Poetry in English. Irish women writers. Anthologies
  I. Henry, P. L. (Patrick Leo)
  821.00809287

ISBN 0 85342 956 1 *Hardback*
ISBN 0 85342 955 3 *Paperback*

Printed in Ireland by Colour Books Ltd

Contents

Preface		7
Introduction		9

EARLY IRISH POEMS, MAXIMS AND TRIADS

1. *Deirdre* – The Birth of Deirdre — 26
2. *Óenét Emire* – The Only Jealousy of Emer — 28
3. *Echtra Condla* – The Voyage of Connla — 32
4. *Ad-Muiniur Secht n-Ingena* – I Invoke the Seven Daughters — 38
5. *Aithbe Dam Cen Bés Mora* – Lament of the Old Woman of Beare — 40
6. *Slán Seiss, A Brigit Co mBúaid* – Victorious Brigit I — 46
7. *Brigit Buadach* – Victorious Brigit II — 50
8. *Comrac Líadaine Ocus Cuirithir* – Líadan and Cuirithir — 52
9. *Bennacht Fort* – A Blessing on Thee — 60
10. *Fingal Rónáin* – Rónán's Lament — 62
11. *Reicne Fothaid Canainne* – Fothad Canainne's Poem: The Fatal Tryst — 66
12. *It É Saigte Gona Súain* – Créd's Lament — 72
13. *Tecosca Cormaic* – The Instructions of Cormac — 74
14. *Trecheng Breth Féni* – The Triads of Ireland — 76
15. *Mé Éba* – I am Eve — 80
16. *Ciodh Ma nDeilighe* – Why Do You Part Me? — 80
17. *A Bhean Lán de Stuaim* – O Woman Full of Grace — 84
18. *Ní Bhfuighe Mise Bás Duit* – I Shall Not Die for Thee — 86
19. *'Sí Mo Ghrádh* – My Love — 88
20. *Léig Díot t'Airm* – Lay Down Your Arms — 88

MODERN IRISH TRIADS AND PROVERBS

21. *Tréanna* – Modern Irish Triads — 94
22. *Seanfhocail na Muimhneach* – Munster Proverbs — 96
23. *Seanfhocla Chonnacht* – Connacht Proverbs — 100
24. *Seanfhocla Uladh* – Ulster Proverbs — 104

MODERN IRISH SONGS AND POEMS

25. *A Ógánaigh an Chúil Cheangailte* – O Youth of the Loose-Bound Hair — 110

26. *Dónall Óg* – Donal Óg   112
27. *Caiseal Mumhan* – Cashel of Munster or
    An Clár Bog Déil – The Soft Deal Board   116
28. *A Bhuachaill an Chúil Dualaigh* – O Youth of the
    Ringlets   116
29. *An Cuimhin Leat an Oíche Úd?* – You Remember
    that Night?   118
30. *Máirín de Barra*   120
31. *Bean an Fhir Rua* – The Wife of the Red-Haired Man   122
32. *Mala Néifinn* – The Brow of Nephin   126
33. *An Seanduine* – The Old Man   128
34. *Iníon an Phailitínigh* – The Palatine's Daughter   130
35. *Snaidhm an Ghrá* – The Love Knot   132
36. *Caoineadh na dTrí Muire* – Lament of the Three
    Marys   134
37. *Mo Bhrón ar an bhFarraige* – My Grief on the Sea   138
38. *Droimeann Donn Dílis* – Dear Brown Drimmin   140
39. *An Chúileann* – The Coolin   142
40. *Ceann Dubh Dílis* – Dear Dark Head   142
41. *Cúnla*   144
42. *Caoineadh Airt Uí Laoghaire* – Lament for Art
    O Leary   146
43. *Cúirt an Mheán Oíche* – The Midnight Court   158
44. *Má's Buairt Rómhór* – If 'Twas Too Great a Sadness   194
45. *Gein Nár Milleadh* – The Unaborted   196
46. *Caoineadh* – Lament   200
47. *Finit*   202
48. *Labhrann Deirdre* – Deirdre Speaks   202
49. *Táimid Damanta, a Dheirféaracha* – Sisters, we are
    Damned   204
50. *Féar Suaithinseach* – Special Grass   208
51. *A Chroí Tincéara* – O Heart of a Tinker   210

Abbreviations   214
Bibliographical   215
Acknowledgements   217

Preface

My object in this anthology is to bring together from the successive phases of Irish civilisation memorable poems in which women, or the female principle, figure, either as a potent cause of poetry, or in the working out of poems. Hence the net is flung widely. Placing the woman firmly in the centre of the picture probably occasions a bias in her favour and a greater inclusiveness in the anthology, which in itself is a good thing. It may serve as an antidote to the bias in favour of men which has prevailed through much of the world's history, as discussed in the *Introduction.*

The poems range from the oldest phase of Irish civilisation known to us down through Old, Middle and Modern Irish. The oldest phase, called *heroic*, has its own metrical form called *rosc* which is rhythmical, alliterative, rhetorical verse not yet organised in stanzas. It is followed by the Old Irish period from about AD 700-900 during which the 4-lined rhymed stanza of syllabic lines comes into its own.

The so-called Middle Irish period is reckoned from about AD 900 to 1100. It is followed by the period of Bardic poetry and strict metrical rules; this lasts from about 1200 to 1600. After that comes the Modern period when song metres become popular. Scholars would push the Modern Irish period back to the thirteenth century on the grounds that the Irish language in its essentials had reached the modern phase by then.

A distinction is made between the date a poem was composed and the date of the manuscript in which it is written down. The actual manuscripts in which the early poetry survives were written mainly between the twelfth and the seventeenth centuries; in most cases, then, long after the poems were composed and in a later variety of Irish. This gap between composition and transmission provides the chief problem for editors. One can tell when a poem was *composed* by examining the rhyming words, the spellings, the grammar and the word meanings.

To the earliest type, *rosc*, belong Poems *1-3*. Poems *5-12* are Old Irish, rhymed and stanzaic. Between these two kinds is the

7

transitional No. *4*. Old Irish, also, is No. *13*, the *Instructions* of King Cormac to his son. Nos. *15-16* are Middle Irish: No. *16*, a late Middle Irish dramatic chant, is isolated; its unrhymed short verses are reminiscent of short *rosc* verses, as in Nos. *4* and *42*. Old Irish triads are presented in No. *14*, Modern Irish in *21*. Poems *17-20* are Bardic, poems *25-51* Modern.

Early Irish text has been somewhat simplified where possible, but not standardised. Where published editions of Early Irish texts may be compared, it will be seen that in *Dánta Ban* alternative manuscript readings are sometimes preferred and stanzas of lesser interest or less reliable transmission omitted. For some modern poems, such as *41*, and proverbs which are essentially local and dialectal, phonetic rather than standardised forms are used. In some cases, such as *38*, *39*, older orthography in the source is modernised.

In regard to the titles of poems, Irish lyrics are generally designated by their first line, rather than by a special title, although this is less true of the modern period. In providing bilingual titles I have been largely guided by practical needs.

The earlier poetry, like the modern folksong, is mostly anonymous, so that apart from Nos. *9*, *17* and *20*, named poets are found only towards the end of my selection.

I am grateful to my wife, Siobhán, for much help, and to Seán Ó Cinnéide for answering questions on Kerry idiom.

Introduction

The common assumption that in the early Irish heroic or warrior society men were automatically the dominant sex runs counter to a good deal of the evidence. For one thing, the love experience mirrored in early Irish literature reveals a characteristic pattern of courtship in which the woman plays the leading role. A classic example is the tale of Deirdre.[1] Identified at birth by the druid as one destined to bring untold calamity on Ulster, Deirdre was placed under supervision and educated to be a future spouse of King Conchobor's. The sight of a raven drinking the blood of a calf slaughtered in the snow inspires the maturing girl to long for a future husband with black hair, red cheeks and white skin. No sooner is Naoise identified for her as such than she makes her move. The saga describes the encounter as follows:[2]

> While the aforesaid Naoise was alone outside, she quickly stole out to him, as if to go past him, and he did not recognise her.
> 'Beautiful' said he 'is the heifer going past me.'
> 'Heifers,' said she 'are bound to be big where there are no bulls.'
> 'The bull of the province is with you,' he said 'namely, the king of the Ulstermen.'
> 'I would choose between the two of you,' she said 'and I would take a little young bull like you.'
> 'By no means!' said he 'even because of Cathbad's prophecy.'
> 'Do you say that in order to reject me?'
> 'It will indeed be for that reason,' he said.
> With that, she made a leap at him and seized the two ears on his head.
> 'Two ears of shame and derision are these,' said she 'unless you take me away with you!'
> 'Go away from me, woman!' said he.
> 'That you shall have,' said she.

The upshot was, that to save his honour, Naoise and his brothers felt obliged to leave Ulster with Deirdre.

In the Ossianic cycle of Leinster, Gráinne acquires Diarmait in a similar manner.[3] The marriage feast for the elderly Finn mac Cumaill and the young Gráinne had just begun, for she did not demur at the marriage proposal from Finn put before her by her father Cormac, King of Tara. Gráinne offers drugged wine to Finn and to others who might impede her plans. When they are asleep she approaches Oisín and proposes to him as a peer. Oisín declines and she turns to Diarmait, who also refuses. But this time Gráinne insists, placing him under deadly injunctions (*fá gheasa droma draíochta*), so that Diarmait has no option but to elope with her. In the earliest love poems celebrating this romance, Gráinne is the speaker and Diarmait the love object.

In the eighth century saga of Froech (*Táin Bó Fraích*) it is the elfin hero's beauty in the eyes of Medb's daughter Findabair that is described for us, and not the reverse, as we might expect; for Findabair is here the pawn on offer to Froech for his assistance in the expedition against Ulster!

> What Findabair would say ever after when she saw something beautiful, was that she would far rather see Froech coming over the dark pool, his body so bright, his hair so lovely, his face so shapely, his eye so grey, such a gentle youth without fault or flaw, his face broad above, narrow below, and he so straight, unblemished, the branch with red berries between throat and bright face. What Findabair would say: she never saw anything that came to one third or one half of his beauty.[4]

The case of Medb (Maeve) transcends courtship to corroborate very firmly the overriding significance of the woman-figure in early Irish civilisation, as appears from the following (abridged) account:

> My father was High-king of Ireland. He had six daughters, of whom I was the noblest and the most distinguished. I was best in respect of bounty and generosity. I was best in battle and encounter and single combat. I had a large army of my own, and my father gave me the province of Connacht. I was sought in marriage by Finn, King of Leinster, by Coirpre Nia Fer, King of Tara, by Conchobor of Ulster and by Eochaid Bec of Munster; and I accepted none of them. For I demanded an unwonted bride-price – one never asked before of an Irishman by a woman: namely, a man without meanness or jealousy or fear. If my husband were mean we would not be suited, for I am generous in largesse and the bestowal of gifts and it were a slight upon him were I better in these respects than he. It were no slight, if we were both equally generous, provided we were both generous. If my husband were timid we would not suit each other, for I win battles and contests and combats singlehanded, and it were a slight upon my husband that his wife should be more vigorous than he, but to be equally so were no slight, provided we were both vigorous. If my husband were jealous, it would not do either, for I was never without a man in the shadow of another by me.[5] Now I found the man I sought, namely yourself, Ailill son of Ross Ruad of Leinster: you were not stingy, nor jealous, nor

inactive. I gave you terms and bride-price, the best a woman can give, namely apparel for twelve men, a chariot worth 21 female slaves, the width of your face of red gold, and the weight of your left forearm of white bronze. Whatever shame or trouble or botheration you suffer, your compensation or honour-price therefor is the same as mine, for you are a husband depending on a wife's property.[6]

Maeve's account of herself here is intended to rebut Ailill's previous comment which has almost the ring of a legal maxim: *Is maith ben ben dagfhir* (The wife of a nobleman is a woman of worth); that is, her status and property is a reflection of her husband's. By the seventh century when the *Táin Bó Cuailnge* (The Cattle Raid of Cooley) was first written down, this would have become normal; but Brehon law retained the pre-Celtic arrangement Maeve describes, as well as other features favourable to women.

Maeve also appears as a symbol of Gaelic sovereignty. Such a woman, such a queen is figured in some of the archaic poems as offering the chalice to the chosen successor who now drinks the wine of sovereignty. The queen is goddess of the land presiding over the induction of a new king: indeed the word for king or prince, *flaith*, is a secondary development from the word for lordship: *flaith*, a feminine noun; and in the application of this word to the meaning 'prince' it retains its feminine gender at first. Welsh *gwlad* 'country' is the full formal equivalent of Irish *flaith* 'lordship', but it never developed the secondary meaning of 'prince' or 'king'. Etymology offers further support for kingship as a dignity mediated by a woman. Maeve's name, *medb*, is an adjective meaning 'intoxicant, inebriating'. In the case of the sacral king we have the ritual intoxication of sovereignty which is akin to the intoxication and inspiration of the poet. Indo-European *medhu* – 'honey, mead' is in Old Irish *mid*, in Welsh *medd*, in Old English *meodo*, in Sanscrit *mádhu* – 'honey, mead'. Hence the concept of the ministrant goddess is contained in the name *Medb* itself.

The concrete data upon which this symbolic interpretation is based are Maeve's absolute power and her polyandry.[7] Her absolute power appears in her relationship vis-à-vis Ailill: in the vital matter of invading Ulster she sets him aside and picks her own commander-in-chief. In the inventory of movable goods which follows Maeve's account above, Ailill does indeed prove to have the edge – but this is without significance for him though it provides a motive for the war. Ailill reigns in Connacht, he tells us, by virtue of his own mother's rights. We find too that the two chief figures of the Ulster cycle, Conchobor mac Nesa and Cú Chulainn mac Dechtire are named after their mothers, while some pedigrees of Fergus mac Roich treat Roich as the name of his mother.[8] In matrilineal succession the sister's son is a vital factor and we can note the importance of this degree of kinship in the *Táin*, the Arthurian cycle and in one branch of the *mabinogion*. Maternal lineage is traditional in Modern Ireland, too, in the case of a *cliamhain isteach*, for instance: that is, a son-in-law entering his wife's property. If she is Nellie O Donovan, her son may be called Johnny Nellie, her grandson Mick Nellie, her great-grandson Tom Nellie.

Filiation through the mother is attested not only for the Picts of North Britain but also in the early history of the Greeks, Latins and Germans. It need not necessarily imply a significant lack of power on the paternal side. The case of Maeve and Ailill is different. Here Maeve appears as a matriarchal figure. This fact seems to be isolated and vestigial, but it is none the less important and significant, even though she is not a historical figure.

As the invasion of Ulster by Maeve gets under way, all Ulstermen save Cú Chulainn – for he is of the British Setantii – are seized by a weakness which renders them unfit for military service. This is explained in the legend as a reprisal by Macha, the native goddess outraged by the Ulstermen when they took the province from the Cruithin. The men's weakness is interpreted by some scholars as an example of the *couvade*, a form of confinement at childbirth similar to the mother's, observed by men in some primitive societies.[9] It appears from the *Táin* that it was in part a ceremonial presided over by a druid.

'Whatever happens among the gods above' it has been said 'reflects events on earth'. The foregoing facts are reinforced by the overriding importance of symbolic women figures in the life of ancient Ireland. The Gaels have to go and propitiate the tutelary goddesses of Ireland – Éire, Fotla and Banba – before they can claim the land. Similarly, all the ancient sanctuaries of Ireland are associated with women founders: Tara with Tea, Emain Macha with Macha, Tailltiu and Tlachtga with women of the same name. The river Boyne is the goddess Bovinda, reminiscent of Anna Livia Plurabelle of a later time.[10] The goddess Brigantia, representing the lordship of the powerful

Brigantes of North Britain, (of whom Cú Chulainn's tribe, the Setantii,were a sub-sept) is a forerunner of our own Saint Brigit whose name means 'the High one': see poems 6-7. In poem 4 the 'Seven Daughters of the Sea' weave the threads of human destiny; in No. 3 the fairywoman wields supernatural power; and in No. 1 Deirdre becomes a symbol of disaster for Ulster.

Apart from local goddesses, the Celts of Britain and Ireland were deeply concerned with the goddess in her role of divine mother: we have Irish Anu and Danu, British Modron and Don. Modron's son Mabon is known by his mother's name, Mabon vab Modron. The name Mabon is identical with Irish *in Mac Óc*, soubriquet of Oengus, son of the Dagda.

The concepts and patterns of relationship outlined above were part of the total outlook of the Irish people in the eighth and ninth centuries of the Christian era. By that time the pre-Celtic stratum of the population, hailing, according to linguistic and cultural criteria, from the Mediterranean area, had merged with the North European in a mould which has determined the character of rural Gaelic Ireland to our own day, absorbing successive waves of newcomers, Viking, Anglo-Norman, English and Scottish. But from these later settlements, especially in the east of Ireland and in the towns, a different attitude to life and to the relationship of the sexes developed, naturally enough. None of this can be adequately assessed until account is taken of the wider European and Middle Eastern context which contributed so much to it and which provides a yardstick to measure it by.

We begin with the situation in the earliest phase of Indo-European civilisation some 4,000 years ago as mirrored or reflected in the oldest evidence from Greek, and other ancient languages of Europe and Asia. The fact that in the oldest Greek mythology a divine goddess Hera stands undiminished beside the father of the gods, Zeus, marks in reality an adaptation by the invading Achaeans to the great native goddess of Argos which is similar to that of the Gaels to Éire, Fotla and Banba. What happens when this accommodation is not made is clearly seen in the plight of Conchobor's Ulstermen who, for outraging the goddess Macha's prerogatives, were doomed to ritual prostration with which they sought to appease the goddess on the occasion of every great national extremity, such as invasion.

In Mesopotamia and Egypt women were privileged. In the Egypt of the Pharaohs the land belonged to the queen and the

13

king succeeded by marrying the daughter of his predecessor. Brother married sister in order to retain property in the family. The cult of the Egyptian goddess Isis, sister and wife of Osiris, was so active and widespread as to pose a threat to Christianity for the domination of Europe. The Greek epics, meanwhile, show that Greek women had some of the privileges of women in Babylonia and Egypt, notably in the succession to kingship. The relative freedom which women enjoyed forms the background of the exemplary love scene between Hector and Andromache in the sixth book of the *Iliad*.

By the time of Plato's *Symposium* (about 385 BC) we can observe a notable change. In his discussion of love Plato envisages a development in which the young and inexperienced person begins by contemplating physical beauty: he will first fall in love with one particular beautiful person and beget noble sentiments in partnership with him. The love object can be a boy or a man or an activity. The higher love towards which he should later develop is that of beautiful sentiments and ideas. The term *homosexual* with its current connotation of physical or sexual gratification can obstruct the understanding of Plato and of later medieval civilisation. Beside it one needs a word such as *monosexual*, free from such connotation. For example, one of the privileges of the medieval Irish *fili* or poet was to sleep in the bed of his lord and patron; and in some poems the *fili* represents himself as his prince's wife – who may be yearning for another husband. No one has suggested that this literary conceit rests upon homosexual practice. Meanwhile, in so far as the love of man for woman finds a place at all in Plato's scheme, it belongs to the lower level, to 'Common Aphrodite'.

The Hellenic balance to Plato's treatment of love is held by the great sixth century BC poet Sappho whose love poems are addressed to the girls she taught. A girl about to marry whose future seems dark evokes a memorable image:[11]

> Like the wild hyacinth flower that on the hills is found,
> Which the passing feet of the shepherds constantly press down,
> And yet the purple blossom still blooms upon the ground.

Although the adjective *Lesbian* from Lesbos, Sappho's island home, has come to denote female homosexualism, there is no evidence for the attribution of this practice to Sappho herself. If there were, doubtless Aristotle would have put it otherwise when he wrote: 'The people of Lesbos honour Sappho – even though she is a woman.'

Hebrew legend and history commemorate a sequence of great women such as Ruth, Esther, Deborah, Jael, Sarah, Rebecca, Rachel and Judith and the Hebrew myth of the Fall of Man from the Garden of Paradise shows Eve to advantage as inquisitive, lively and active, where Adam is sluggish, diffident and craven: 'The woman whom thou gavest to be with me, she gave me of the tree and I did eat' he pleads. Anti-feminism, which is not yet explicit in Plato, sets in with Saint Paul of Tarsus, who took the myth at face value and believed in an historical Adam and Eve. Sex became equated with original sin, and woman, formed from man according to the myth, should be subject to him and should cover her head in token of subjection. From the seventh century the bias in favour of men is confirmed in Islam, in the Koran.

Anti-feminism flourished in medieval times and was reinforced or renewed in the Christian churches of Britain and Ireland in the eighteenth and nineteenth centuries when morality tended to be equated with sexual morality. The sexual desire itself comes once more under attack, woman's beauty is reduced to an aspect of man's temptation, and much of human life is squeezed through the needle eye of an obsession. A religion of fear replaced Christ's rule of love and clerics, burning in a contorted puritan zeal, detected sin in every move of the human spirit. One is reminded of John Knox's *First Blast of the Trumpet against the Monstrous Regiment of Women* in which woman is a creature 'painted forth by nature to be weak, frail, impatient, feeble and foolish'.

We can now return to the Gaelic tradition and trace it on to modern times in Ireland. We found that by the ninth century, Gaelic and pre-Gaelic attitudes to the relationship of the sexes had merged and the position of women was quite favourable. The account of Medb's courtship and marriage above from the Book of Leinster *Táin* was penned in the twelfth century. Ailill's married status was legally that of *fer for bantinchor*, 'a husband without means on his wife's estate'. This is the third type of marriage[12] out of ten mentioned in the Brehon Laws, which are concerned with such a husband's right to contract, the service he must offer in lieu of property, and the share he is entitled to in case of divorce. He is legally the minor party in such a marriage. He is allotted certain rights under the headings mentioned, provided he serves satisfactorily: either by managing such household affairs as the ploughing arrangements, or by guiding

15

wisely and constructively the household deliberations at the domestic planning sessions.[13]

Divorce, available to both sexes, is granted to women on such grounds as a husband's impotence, imbecility, incurable ailment and religious vocation; also on grounds of physical assault, exposure to ridicule, and failure to maintain. The Heptads which contain these provisions show a high regard for women's dignity and rights.[14] Secondary wives are recognised beside a principal wife, and their status, rights and duties are specified. Brehon Law came into conflict with Canon Law in the medieval period: there is mention, for instance, of children and kinsfolk inside some of the Cistercian monasteries in the course of the thirteenth century.[15] Now, according to Brehon Law, if the father of a child were a cleric, i.e. a priest, monk or bishop, he would become liable under certain circumstances for its education, which probably accounts for the presence of children in the monasteries. Clerical celibacy, it should be noted, was not a feature of the earlier Irish Church; the champions of Canon law, however, tended to treat deviations from the Roman system as abuses, whatever their historical justification might be.

The poetry of the period 1200-1600 represents a blend of two aristocracies, the professional order of native bards lending a traditional metrical form to the life experience or conventional sentiment of the Norman-Gaelic lords, whose inspiration often came from outside. The polish of this courtly poetry can raise a doubt about its sincerity of feeling. But there is exceptional achievement, too, as when the sixteenth century Domhnall mac Carthaigh, Earl of Clancarthy, a good poet with a religious vein, addresses his love plaint to Heaven:[16]

Amhrán a béil,	The song of her lips –
Bile mar rós,	Like a rose tree she,
Milis mar thúis,	As incense sweet! –
Do chuir mé ar buile báis,	Has put me in death frenzy,
Cá cruinne cúis?	What cause more just?

The West-Kerry poet Piaras Feiritéar composes with elegance in the same vein (See Poem No. 20).

Typical, too, is the manner of the sixteenth century Cúchonnacht Ó Cléirigh, whose swan image here does not unduly tax his invention:[17]

Do chongaib mé m'fheóil is m'fhuil,
Do ghrádh ainnre an chuirp mar ghéis;
Ithim mórán, do-ním suan,
In gach ceól is buan mo spéis.

I did not forfeit flesh or blood,
Though I did love her swanlike grace;
I take my fill of sleep and food
And music is my great solace.

Cúchonnacht shares the ironic polished manner with the fourteenth century Gerald the Rimer Fitzgerald, Third Earl of Desmond, one of the most notable early practitioners: as in his poem on women *Mairg adeir olc ris na mnáibh* (Ill-betide the one who speaks ill of women):[18]

Duine arsaidh leathan liath,
Ní hé a mian dul 'na dháil;
Annsa leo an buinneán óg bocht;
Mairg adeir olc ris na mnáibh!

The man that's bulky, old and grey,
Him they have no wish to visit,
The poor young sapling they prefer,
Woe to the one speaks ill of women!

The most notable aspects of Modern Irish verse since 1650 are firstly the folk poetry and secondly the *Aisling* or political vision poems of the eighteenth century in which the beautiful princess Éire bewails her lot and awaits redress through a Stuart prince. The woman figure is indispensable not only to the *Aisling* but also to the major poems of the modern period such as the 'Lament for Art O Leary' (No. 42) and the 'Midnight Court' (No. 43). The former of these, composed by a woman for a husband slain in a feud with a local representative of English law, belongs in form and content to an age-old ritual genre in which the woman has naturally assumed the leading role. The 'Midnight Court' is in effect a symposium of women on the ills of a man-made social system which they seek to adjust in order to find suitable male partners for marriageable girls.

The changeover from classical bardic form, elegant, re-strained and ornate to the more expressive – sometimes rollick-ing – assonantal patterns of the modern *Amhrán* or Song metres marks a thoroughgoing change of climate. Not that transitional figures like Piaras Feiritéar were lacking who could compose in

17

the new as in the older manner. But the move is from an aristocratic – and doomed – order to a dispossessed and classless native society nourishing their poetic tradition in scattered schools of poetry and finding models where they could. The transition is well-marked in the poems of the early seventeenth century Mathghamhain Ó hIfearnáin: *A mhic, ná meabhraigh éigse!* (My son, do not cultivate the poetic art!) and *Ceist! cia do cheinneóchadh dán?* (Tell me, who will buy a poem?). Of the same period, Eochaid Ó hEóghusa, poet of the Maguires of Fermanagh, writes in lighter, mocking vein of the change in literary fashions to 'a common sort of easy art which brings me more praise' (*ar shórt gnáthach grés robhog / is mó as a moltar sinde.*[19]

> Do thréig mé – gá mó sonas? –
> mo slighthe docra diamhra:
> dá cluine cuid dar ndáinne,
> Beanfaidh gáire as an iarla.

> I have abandoned – what greater luck? –
> My hard mysterious ways:
> If he hear some of my verse,
> It will make the Earl laugh.

The downfall of the native nobility brought with it the immediate decline of its representative literary culture.

Arising out of this, we find a change of stance towards the beloved in popular love poetry. Where the sophisticated mind and conventional metre of the aristocratic court poet produced a polished poem reflecting the social graces, the peasant poet, who is neither uncultured nor without sensibility, and who has a keen eye for the detail, reaches out directly for simple and telling words to pattern the mood of his poem or the emotion of his song. The basis or principle underlying the organisation of emotional detail is found in the texture of the love relationship. In a poem such as *Dónall Óg* (No. 26) a complete pattern of relationship and involvement with the beloved is traced out culminating in a remarkable final stanza:

> Do bhainis soir dhíom, is do bhainis siar dhíom,
> Do bhainis romham is do bhainis im' dhiaidh dhíom,
> Do bhainis gealach is do bhainis grian díom,
> 'S is rómhór m'eagla gur bhainis Dia dhíom.

> You've taken east from me, you've taken west from me,
> The road behind me and the road before,

You've taken moon, you've taken sun from me,
And I'm in dread you've taken the God I adore.

The cosmic proportion of love is found again – directly and instinctively – in No. *37*.

Mo bhrón ar an bhfarraige,
Is í atá mór,
's í ag gabháil idir mé
Is mo mhíle stór.

My grief on the sea,
How massively it rolls!
For it comes between me
And the love of my soul.

The sea is not vaster than the love which seeks to transcend it in order to find its object. Spontaneous expression is the virtue of this poetry with its unerringly right because inevitable formulations, as if the poem were directly mediated by the Muse, rather than fabricated.

Of the same kind as these poems is the impressive *Máirín de Barra*, No. *30*, except that here the *persona* is a man and the beloved a woman. This poem owes its greater tension to the several forms of repetitive device employed, particularly to the kind called parallelism where phrases or verses of like structure follow one another in sequence:

Do shíl mé thú 'mhealladh le briathra 's le póga,
Do shíl mé thú 'mhealladh le leabhartha 's le móide,
Do shíl mé thú 'mhealladh ar bhreacadh na heornan,
Ach d'fhág tú dubhach dealabh ar theacht don mbliain nó mé.

I thought to beguile you with words and with kisses,
I thought to beguile you with books, with promises,
I thought to beguile you when the barley had ripened
But you left me sad and dreary at the New Year's arrival.

The genre structure of the modern Irish folksong of love can be largely defined in terms of French categories.[20] In first place comes the *chanson d'amour*, a love-song addressed by a man to his beloved, as *Caiseal Mumhan* (No. *27*), *Máirín de Barra* (*30*), *Bean an Fhir Rua* (*31*), *Mala Néifinn* (*32*), *Ceann Dubh Dílis* (*40*). Next the *chanson de jeune fille* which the love-lorn girl directs to her beloved as in *A Ógánaigh an Chúil Cheangailte* (*25*), *Dónall Óg* (*26*), *A Bhuachaill an Chúil Dualaigh* (*28*), *Mo Bhrón ar an bhFarraige* (*37*). The *chanson dialoguée* is a conversation between

19

the two as in Nos. *34, 35: Iníon an Phailitínigh* and *Snaidhm an Ghrá*. Then there is the *chanson de malmariée* which the unsuitably wed young woman directs at her old husband, e.g. No. *33, An Seanduine*. No. *41, Cúnla* is a burlesque form of the serenade in which the young woman yields to her lover's entreaty to enter her house, and the intriguing No. *39, An Chúileann*, resembles a *reverdie* in its visionary impression of an encounter with a girl early on a fine bright morning. No. *29, An Cuimhin Leat an Oíche Úd?*, is an example of the *aube*, in which dawn parts the lovers. Besides, that remarkable poem *Cúirt an Mheán Oíche* (No. *43*) has the general framework of the medieval southern French *cours d'amour* or courts of the nobility in which love problems were debated and resolved. In the *Cúirt* the controversy proceeds by *débat* or debate between a young woman and an old man. Part I of this poem is a *complainte* in which the girl complains she has no husband, while Part III is built around a *chanson de malmariée* figuring the grievances of the young wife combined with a burlesque account of the old man's impotence.

Some features of *amour courtois* are found in Modern Irish love songs which are absent from the bardic poems preceding them. We may mention first the troubadour attitude to love as represented in Don Quixote's formulation 'a knight-errant without a mistress was a tree without either fruit or leaves, and a body without a soul'.[21] Compare the last stanza of No. *32* where the one deprived of love is associated with the ebbing tide and likened to 'a tree on the mountain side/forsaken by its bloom'. The preceding stanza of the same poem illustrates a second courtly feature: the contrast between the deprived lover and uninhibited, joyful nature around him: 'How happy for the little birds/That soar aloft so high/And sleep together/On the one little bough./This happiness is not for me/And the one love of my life...' Two notable characteristics of *amour courtois* are the requirement of secrecy and the absolute perfection of the beloved: she is a paragon, especially of beauty. Compare No. *27*, stanza 3: *Searc mo chléibh a thug mé féin duit is grá trí rún* (All my love I gave to you, from the world concealed); and No. *30*, stanza 4 on the pattern *Is aoibhinn don talamh a siúlann tú féin air* (Happy the ground where your own two feet tread). For the courtly poet it follows that a kiss from the lips of such a one, or acceptance by her, is the lover's only cure. See No. *31*, stanza 4:

'Sé mo shólás go bás, is é d'fháil ó fhlaitheas anuas,

20

Aon phóigín amháin, is é d'fháil ó bhean an fhir ruaidh.

'Tis my solace till death to receive down from Heaven the delight
Of one kiss from the lips of my darling the Red Man's Wife.

Also No. *30*, stanza 5:

'S go dtógfá ón mbás mé ach a rá gur leat féin mé.

And you'd save me from death by just saying that I'm yours.

The beloved is preferred, as often in Provence, to the promise of
Heaven: No. *35*, stanza 4:

'Dtaobh gan amhras gur bh'fhearr liom agam tu
Ná'n dá asbal déag, is ná maor an anama.

Although indeed I would rather you
Than the twelve apostles, or the guardian of the soul.

Finally, we may mention the motif of the beloved in church or
chapel who comes between the lover and his or her prayers: No.
30, stanza 2:

Do thugas 's do thugas 's do thugas óm chroí greann duit,
Ar maidin lae'l Muire na gcoinneal sa teampall.

From the depths of my heart all my love to you I gave
On that morning in the chapel at the feast of the Presentation.

Also, No. *26*, *Dónall Óg*, Stanza 11:

Siúd é an Domhnach do thugas grá duit,
An Domhnach díreach roimh Domhnach Cásca,
Is mise ar mo ghlúinibh ag léamh na Páise,
Sea bhí mo dhá shúil ag síor-thabhairt an ghrá dhuit.

That was the Sunday I gave my love to your keeping,
At the mass of the Palms before Sunday of Easter,
Christ's Passion of branches on my knees I was reading,
But my two eyes were on you and my heart was bleeding.

Modern poems on our list which fall outside the French
categories used above are the two Laments, Nos. *36* and *42*, the
Jacobite political song, No. *38* and Nos. *44-51*. No. *44* recalls a
dimension of natural magic among the Celts with its inventory
of scenic places which can cure the sick human spirit: at one time
merely naming them in a poem would have been calculated to
produce results. Eibhlín Ní Mhurchú's poem on the generation
gap, No. *45*, is not only well-wrought and memorable, but also
a significant social document.

Nos. *46-48* from Máire Mhac an tSaoi's *An Cion go dtí Seo* of 1987 and Nos. *49-51* from Nuala Ní Dhomhnaill's *Féar Suaithinseach* of 1984 are our remaining representatives from the twentieth century. One of the most impressive and engaging lyric voices of her time, Máire Mhac an tSaoi welds together strands of emotion, intellect and complex background, folk and literary, into a rare unity. In every sense modern, her poems reflect also in part the formal fastidiousness and thematic interests of historic Irish-Gaelic poetry – as in No. *48*, which links up with our opening poem on Deirdre.

Nuala Ní Dhomhnaill is one of our most distinguished younger poets in Irish. She shares with Eibhlín and Máire a mastery of her idiom, West Kerry Irish, and a keen interest in folklore, which becomes in fact a staple of her muse – as in No. *50*. This serves as an anchor, for the younger generation has in the meantime become 'liberated'. In Nuala's poems of open reference (as in Nos. *49, 51*) the old acquiescence and romantic idealism have yielded to a mobile, if not picaresque realism: in all, a very contemporary and international trend.

NOTES

1. See Poem No. *1*, p. 26.
2. See V. Hull, ed., *Longes mac n-Uislenn*, Oxford, 1949, p. 46.
3. S. H. O'Grady, ed. *Tóruigheacht Dhiarmuda agus Ghráinne*, Trans. of the Ossianic Society 1855, Vol. III, Dublin, 1857, p. 52 ff.
4. See W. Meid, ed. *Táin Bó Fraích*, Dublin, 1974, p. 8.
5. I.e. I was never without one lover quickly succeeding another.
6. See R. I. Best & M. A. O'Brien, ed. *The Book of Leinster* II, Dublin, 1956, pp. 261-2.
7. This is described in the tale with the apt title 'Maeve's Share of Husbands'.
8. See *Corp. Gen.* p. 336, *Cóir Anmann* 282. Others would take *Roig/ Roich* from *Ro-ech*.
9. See P. L. Henry, *Saoithiúlacht na Sean-Ghaeilge*, Dublin, 1976, pp. 28-39.
10. Anna Livia < Abha na Life 'The river Liffey'.
11. See J. M. Edmonds, ed. *Lyra Graeca* I, Loeb, 1922, p. 288.
12. It is less frequent than the marriage in which both parties have the status of contributors of wealth, the *lánamnas comthinchuir*. Note that *cétmuinter* 'head of the household, chief spouse', applicable to either husband or wife, generally refers to the latter.
13. R. Thurneysen et al., *Studies in Early Irish Law*, Dublin, 1936, pp. 16, 57-59.
14. *Ibid.*, 240-257.
15. See *Studia Hibernica* 12, 1972, p. 136 ff.
16. DG, p. 39.

17. DG, p. 10.
18. DG, p. 4.
19. O. Bergin, *Irish Bardic Poetry*, Dublin, 1970, p. 127.
20. See S. Ó Tuama, *An Grá in Amhráin na nDaoine*, Dublin, 1960.
21. See A. Jeanroy, *La Poésie Lyrique des Troubadours* I, Paris, 1934, p. 95.

Early Irish Poems, Maxims and Triads

1. Deirdre

Bátar Ulaid oc ól i taig Fheidlimthe maic Daill, scélaigi Conchobuir. Baí dano ben ind Fheidlimthe oc airiuc don t-slúag ósa cinn is sí thorrach.Tairmchell corn ocus chuibrenn ocus ro-lásat gáir mesca. A mbátar do lepthugud, do-lluid in ben dia lepaid. Oc dul dí dar lár in taige, ro-gréch in lenab inna broinn co-closs fon less uile. At-raig cach fer di alailiu is'tig lasin scréich í-sin co-mbátar cinn ar chinn isin tig. Is and ad-ragart Sencha mac Ailella:

'Na cuirid cor díb!' or-se.' Tucthar cucunn in ben co-festar cid dia-tá a ndeilm se.'

Tucad íarum in ben chucu. Is and as-bert a céile, Feidlimid:

Cía deilm dremun derdrethar,
Dremnas fot broinn búredaig?
Bruith cluasaib cluinethar
Gloim eter do dá thoíb, trén-tormaid.
Mór n-úath adn-áigethar
Mo chride créchtnaigther crúaid.

Is and ro-lá-si co Cathbad, ar ba fissid side:

Cluinid Cathbad coím-ainech,
Caín-mál, mind mór mochtaide
Mbrogthar tre druidechta drúad,
Ór nad-fil lem féin find-fhocla
Fris-mberad Feidlimid
Fursundud fiss,
Ar nad-fitir ban-scál
Cía fo brú bí,
Cid fom chriol bronn bécestar.

Is and as-bert Cathbad:

Fot chriol bronn bécestair
Bé fuilt buidi buide-chass
Ségdaib súilib sell-glassaib.
Sían a grúade gorm-chorcrai,

1. The Birth of Deirdre

Deirdre, the great tragic heroine of Irish literature, figures centrally in one of the best sagas of the Ulster Cycle, Longas mac n-Uislenn The Exile of the Sons of Uisliu, *which was composed in the ninth or tenth century. Here, from the beginning of the saga, is part of the account of her birth.*

The Ulstermen were drinking in the house of Feidlimid mac Daill, Connor's storyteller. Now, Feidlimid's wife was standing over the (reclining) host, serving them, and she pregnant. Drinking-horns and portions of food were being passed around and they raised a drunken cry. When they were about to go to bed, the woman came towards her bed. While she was going across the middle of the house, the child in her womb screamed so that it was heard throughout the whole enclosure. At that scream each man within rose up from the other so that they were face to face in the house. Then Sencha mac Ailella[1] called out: 'Don't stir,' said he. 'Let the woman be brought to us, that it may be known what is the cause of this noise.'

Thereupon the woman was brought to them. Then her husband, Feidlimid, said:

> What frantic noise resounds,
> Raging in your bellowing womb?
> It crushes the ears of the hearer.
> The clamour of your sides resounds mightily.
> Fearing great horrors
> My heart is grievously wounded.

Then she rushed to Cathbad, for he was a seer:

> Hear Cathbad of the comely face,
> A fair prince, a great mighty diadem,
> Who is magnified by druid arts,
> For I myself have no true words
> From which Feidlimid might obtain
> Enlightenment of knowledge;
> For a woman does not know
> Who is in her quick womb,
> Or what cried out in the casket of my womb.

Then Cathbad said:

> In the casket of your womb cried
> A woman with curly yellow hair,
> With fine blue-grey eyes;
> Like the foxglove her pink-purple cheeks,

27

Fri dath snechtai samlamar
Sét a détgne díanim;
Niamdai a beoil partuing-deirg,
Bé dia-mbiat il-ardbe
Eter Ulad erredaib.

2. Óenét Emire

Fand (le Loeg): Fég, a Loíg, dar th'éis!
Oc coistecht frit filet mná cóiri cíallmaithi
co scenaib glasgéraib ina ndeslámaib,
co n-ór fria n-uchtbruinnib.
Cruth caín at-chíchither
amal tecait láith gaile dar cathchairptiu.
Glé ro soí gné Emer ingen Forgaill.

Cú Chulainn (le Fand): Nít ágara, ocus nícon tora etir.
Tairsiu isin creit cumachta
lasin suidi ngríanda form dreichse fo-déin,
Ar do thesarcoin-siu ar andrib ilib imdaib
i cetharaird Ulad,
ar cía nos báigea ingen Fhorgaill
a hucht a comalta im gním co cumachta,
bés ní lim lámathar.

(le hEmir): Not sechnaim-se, a ben,
amal shechnas cách a chárait,
Ním rubai-se do gae crúaid crithlámach,
ná do scían tím thanaide,
ná t'fherg thréith thimaircthech,
ar is mórdoilig mo nert
do scor ó niurt mná.

To the hue of snow I compare
The spotless jewels of her teeth;
Lustrous her lips scarlet-red;
For her many Ulster chariot fighters
Will find a gory bed.

1. The wise counsellor among Connor's Ulstermen

2. The Only Jealousy of Emer

This scene is taken from the romance called 'The Sick-bed of Cú Chulainn'
(Serglige Con Culainn) *in which the hero becomes involved with a fairy-*
woman, Fand. When the hero trysts with her at Newry, he and his charioteer
Loeg are surprised by Cú Chulainn's wife, Emer, who is accompanied by fifty
women armed with knives. The following conversation in the traditional
'rhetorical' style of the poets then takes place:

Fand (to Loeg): Look behind you, Loeg!
    Well-proportioned, sensible women are listening to you
    With sharp grey knives in their right hands
    And gold on their breasts.
    A beautiful sight you will see,
    Like champions coming over war-chariots.
    Clearly Emer, daughter of Forgall, has changed counten-
        ance.

Cú Chulainn (to Fand): Fear not and she will not approach at all.
    Come and sit before me
    In the great chariot with the sunny seat,
    That I may protect you from all the many women
    In the four quarters of Ulster;
    For although Forgall's daughter threaten a mighty deed
    In the midst of her company,
    Perhaps, with me, she will not dare.

(to Emer): Woman, I shun you,
    As everyman shuns his yoke.
    The hard spear in your trembling hand cannot wound me,
    Nor your feeble, thin dagger,
    Nor your anger restrained and weak,
    For it is very difficult for a woman's strength
    To hold my strength in check.

29

Emer: Ceist tra, cid fod-rúair latsu, a Chú Chulainn,
mo dímíad-sa fíad aindrib ilib in chúicid,
ocus fíad aindrib ilib na hÉrenn,
ocus fíad aís einig ar-chena?
Ar is fót chlith tánac-sa,
ocus fo ollbríg do thairisen,
ar cía not báigea úall ollimresan,
bés nípad rith lat-su mo lécun-sa,
a gillai, cía no tríalltá.

Cú Chulainn: Ceist trá, a Emer,
cid arná léicfideá dam-sa
mo denus i ndáil mná?
Ar chétus in bensa,
is sí in glan genmnaid,
gel gasta dingbála do ríg.
Ilchrothach ind ingen sin
do thonnaib dar leraib lánmoraib,
co ndeilb ocus écosc ocus soerchenél,
co ndruini ocus lámda ocus lámthorud,
co céill ocus chonn ocus chobsaidecht,
co n-immad ech ocus bótháinte.
Ar ní fil fo nim
ní bad tol ria coimchéile
ná dingned cía no comgelltá.
A Emer, ni foigeba-su curaid caín créchtach
cathbúadach badam fíu-sa.

Emer: Bés nícon fherr in ben día lenai.
Acht chena is álainn cech nderg,
is gel cach nua,
is caín cech n-ard,
is serb cech ngnáth,
cáid cech n-écmais,
is faill cech n-aichnid
co festar cech n-éolas.

Emer: Tell me, then, Cú Chulainn, what caused you
        To humiliate me before so many women of the province,
        And before many women of Ireland
        And before all honourable people?
        For 'twas under your protection I came
        And under the full power of your guarantee.
        And though the pride of mighty conflict may puff you up,
        Perhaps you might not succeed in abandoning me,
        My lad, even if you tried.

Cú Chulainn : And tell me, Emer,
        Why would you not let me have
        My trysting day with a woman?
        For, first of all, this woman
        Is pure and chaste,
        Bright and clever, a match for a king.
        The girl is very comely,
        She hails from lands over great tidal seas,
        She has form and appearance and is of noble kin,
        Skilled in embroidery, handiwork, handicraft,
        With sense and reason and stability,
        With many horses and herds of cattle.
        For there is nothing under heaven
        The spouse of her bosom might desire
        That she would not do – if you agreed.
        Ah, Emer, you will never find a handsome
        Wound-dealing, conquering champion like me.

Emer: Perhaps the woman you're after is no whit better.
        But, indeed, everything red is beautiful,
        Everything new is bright,
        Every summit delights,
        Everything usual palls,
        Everything absent's revered,
        Everything known is thrown aside
        Until all knowledge is known aright.

3. Echtra Condla (LU)[1]

Lá ro boí Condla Rúad mac Cuind Chétchathaig for láim a athar i n-uachtor Usnig. Co n-acca in mnaí i n-étuch anetargnaid na dochum. As-bert Condla:
'Can do-deochad, a ben?'

'Do-deochad-sa
A tírib beó
Áit inná bí bás
Nó peccad ná immormus.
Do-melom fleda búana cen fhrithgnom.
Caínchomrac linn cen debaid.
Síd mór i taam
Conid de suidiu nonn-ainmnigther áes Síde.'

'Cia, a gillai (ol Cond fria mac) acailli?' Uair ní acca nech in mnaí acht Condla a oenur. Ro fhrecair in ben:

Ad-gládadar
Mnaí n-óic n-álaind sochenéoil
Nad-fresci bás ná sentaid.
Ro-carus Condla Rúad,
Cotn-gairim do Maig mell
Inid rí Bóadag bithsuthain,
Rí cen gol cen mairg inna thír
Ó gabais flaith.

Tair lim
A Chondlai Rúaid muinbricc caindeldeircc,
Barrbude fordot-tá óas gnúis corcorda
Bid ordan do rígdelbae.
Ma chotum-éitis,
Ní crínfa do delb a hoítiu a háldi
Co bráth brindach.

3. The Voyage of Connla

Two areas of early Irish civilisation in which the female principle plays a central role are those of faerie and of political symbolism.[2] *In the* Voyage of Connla *we find a very sensitive treatment of the love theme, as the bond between son and royal father proves too weak against the blandishments of the fairy lover. The* Voyage of Connla *is one of the earliest of Irish tales, going back to the seventh or eighth century. It is a good example of the class, showing a thread of later narrative connecting the older nuclei of poetry.*

One day Connla Rúad,[3] son of Conn of the Hundred Battles was beside his father on the top of Uisnech (in Westmeath). He saw a woman in strange dress approaching him. Connla said:
'Whence have you come, lady?'

'I have come
From lands of immortals,
Where there is no death,
Nor sin nor crime.
We enjoy lasting feasts without exertion.
We have peace without strife,
In a great fairy-mound (or *shee*) we live,
So that therefore we are called people of the *shee*.'

'To whom are you speaking, lad?' said Conn to his son. For no one saw the woman except Connla only. The woman replied:

He speaks
To a beautiful young woman of noble birth,
Who expects neither death nor old age.
I have loved Connla Rúad,
I call him to the Plain of Delights
In which everliving Boadach[4] is king,
King without weeping, without woe in his land,
Since he took kingship.

Come with me,
Connla Rúad of the freckled neck and shining red cheek,
The yellow crown upon you over your crimson face
Is the sovereign sign of your regal figure.[5]
If you come with me, your shape
Will ne'er wither from youth and beauty
Until the visionary doom.

II

As-bert Cond fria druid, Corann a ainm side, ar ro-chualatar uili
an ro-ráidi in ben cenco n-accatar:

Not-álim, a Chorainn
Mórchétlaig, mórdánaig,
Forband dodom-ánic
As-dom mó airli,
As-dom mó cumachtu;
Níth nachim-thánic
Ó gabsu flaith.

Móu imchomruc
Delb nemaicside,
Cotom-éicnigedar immum mac rochaín
D'airchelad tre thóathbandu;
Di láim rígdai
Brechtu ban mberir.

Do-chachain iarom in druí forsin nguth inna mná connach cuala
nech guth na mná ocus conna-accai Condla in mnaí ónd uair sin.
In tan tra luide in ben ass re rochetul in druad, do-chorastar ubull
do Chondlu. Boí Condla co cend mís cen dig cen biad. Nírbu fíu
leis nach túara aile do thomailt acht a ubull. Ní dígbad ní dia ubull
cacha tomled de acht ba ógshlán beus.

III

Gabais eólchaire iarum inní Condla imon mnaí ad-connairc. A llá
ba lán a mí boí for láim a athar i mMaig Archommin intí Condla
co n-acca chuci in mnaí cétnai, a n-as-mbert fris:

Nall suide saides Condla
Eter marbu duthaini
Oc indnaidiu éca úathmair.
Tot-chuiretar bí bithbí,
At-gérat do daínib Tethrach,
Ardot-chiat cach dia
I ndálaib t'athardai

II. Conn's Appeal

Conn spoke to his druid – Corann was his name – for all had heard
what the woman said, though they had not seen her:

> I pray thee, O Corann,
> Great singer, highly gifted,
> A constraint is upon me,
> Exceeding my counsel,
> Exceeding my power,
> A struggle I've not met with
> Since I became king.
>
> Greater in battle,
> the invisible figure
> Overbears me to steal my beloved son
> By wicked wiles away;
> From a royal hand
> He is taken by women's spells.

Then the druid sang upon the woman's voice so that no one heard
her voice and that Connla lost sight of her from that time. As she
was leaving by reason of the druid's incantation, the woman threw
an apple to Connla. Connla went without drink or food for the
space of a month. He didn't think it worth while to partake of any
other food but his apple. However much he ate of this it did not
diminish a whit but remained whole.

III. Connla's Longing

Then longing seized Connla for the woman he had seen. On the
last day of the month he was beside his father on the Plain of
Archommin when he saw the same woman approaching, and she
said to him:

> On the high seat sits Connla
> Among short-lived mortals,
> Awaiting dreadful death.
> The everliving immortals invite you,
> They will call you to the people of Tethra.[6]
> Every day they see you before them
> In the assemblies of your native land

Eter do gnáthu inmaini...

Ba ingnad tra la Cond nicon taibred Condla aithesc do neoch acht tísed in ben.

'In-deochaid fot menmain-siu a rádas in ben, a Chondlai,' ol Cond.

As-bert Condla:

'Ní réid dam, sech caraim mo doíni. Rom-gab dano eólchaire immon mnaí.'

Ro frecart in ben co n-epert:

Táthut − airiunsu rálaib −
Fri toind t'eólchaire óadib
Im loing glano cond-rísmais
Ma ro-ísmais síd Boadaig.

Fil tír n-aill
Nadbu messu do saigid,
At-chíu tairinnith in ngréin,
 Cid céin ricfam ria n-adaig.

Is ed a tír subathar
Menmain cáich dod-imchella,
Ní-fil cenél and nammá
Acht mná ocus ingena.

Fo-ceird Condla iar suidiu bedg úadib co m-boí isind noí glano. Ata-condarcatar uadib. Mod nad mod rond-ísed a súil imram maro do-génsat. Ní-aiccessa ó sin i-lle.

Among the friends you hold dear...

Conn thought it strange that Connla would not reply to anyone save when the woman came.

'Have you taken to heart what the woman says?' asked Conn. Connla said:

'It is not easy for me, for I love my own people. However, a longing for the woman has seized upon me.'

The woman answered and said:
  You are granted the greatest of boons:
  To depart from them to the land of your longing
  In my crystal boat, till we reach
  – If we reach – the *shee* of Boadag.

  There is another land
  Which is no worse to seek,
  I see it, the sun sets,
  Though distant, we'll reach it before night.

  It is the land which pleases
  The mind of all who go round it,
  No other people are there
  Save only women and girls.

Then Connla sprang away from them into the crystal boat. The people saw them receding. Scarcely could their eye follow them as they rowed away on the sea. They have never been seen since.

1. Collated with the other manuscripts.
2. See Introduction, pages 11 and 17.
3. Connla the Red.
4. I.e. *Buadach* 'Victorious' = Welsh *Buddug* as in the name of the British queen Boudicca (Boadicea).
5. Yellow is an otherworld colour.
6. God of the sea.

4. Ad-Muiniur Secht n-Ingena

Ad-muiniur secht n-ingena trethan
dolbtae snáithi macc n-áesmar.
Trí bás úaimm ro-ucaiter,
trí áes dom do-rataiter,
secht tonna tocaid dom do-ro-dáilter!
Ním chollet messe fom chúairt
i llúirig Lasréin cen léiniud!
Ní nassar mo chlú ar chel!
dom-í áes;
ním thí bás comba sen!

Ad-muiniur m'Argetnia
nád bá nád bebe;
amser dom do-r-indnastar
findruini febe!
Ro orthar mo richt,
ro saerthar mo recht,
ro mórthar mo nert,
níp ellam mo lecht,
ním thí bás for fecht,
ro fírthar mo thecht!
Ním ragba nathair díchonn,
ná dorb dúrglass,
ná doel díchuinn!
Ním millither téol,
ná cuire ban,
ná cuire buiden!
Dom-í urchar n-aimsire
ó Ríg inna n-uile!

4. I Invoke the Seven Daughters

This poem is a prayer to pagan divinities for a long life, good fortune and a good reputation. It also requests protection against the hazards which the individual expects to face in the journey through life. The notion of a prayer as a breastplate or armour which protects the speaker from evil was developed in a special way by the Irish, who borrowed the Latin word lorica *'armour' in the form* lúirech, *signifying 'protective prayer'.*

Christian and pagan elements lie side by side in the poem, which is reminiscent of the wide variety of charms known as orthaí *in modern Irish. The poem is attributed to the eighth century abbot of Conry, Co. Westmeath, Fer fio macc Fabri.*

I invoke the seven daughters of the Sea
Who fashion the threads of the sons of long life.
May three deaths be removed from me,
Three lifetimes granted to me,
Seven waves of good fortune conferred on me!
May phantoms not harm me on my journey
In S. Laserian's corslet without hindrance!
May my name not be pledged in vain!
May old age come to me!
May death not come to me until I am old!

I invoke my Silver Champion
Who dies not, who will not die;
May a time be granted me
Of the excellence of white bronze!
May my form be arranged,
May my right be exalted,
May my strength be increased,
May my tomb not be readied,
May I not die on my journey,
May my return be confirmed!
May the headless serpent not seize me,
Nor the hard grey worm,
Nor the senseless chafer!
May no thief harm me,
Nor band of women,
Nor warrior band!
May increase of time come to me
From the King of the Universe!

Ad-muiniur Senach secht aimserach
con-altatar mná síde
for bruinnib búais.
Ní báitter mo shechtchaindel!
Am dún díthogail,
am ail anscuichthe,
am lia lógmar,
am sén sechtmaínech.
Roba chétach,
cétbliadnach,
cach cét diib ar úair.

Cota-gaur cucum mo lessa;
ro bé rath in Spiurto Noíb formsa.
Domini est salus.
Christi est salus.
Super populum tuum, Domine, benedictio tua.

5. Aithbe Dam Cen Bés Mora

Aithbe dam cen bés mora,
sentu fom-dera croan;
toirsi oca cía do-gnéo,
sona do-tét a loan.

Is mé Caillech Bérri, Buí,
no meilinn léini mbithnuí;
in-diu táthum dom shéimi
ná melainn cid aithléini.

It moíni
cartar lib, nídat doíni;

I invoke seven-cycled Senach
Whom fairywomen suckled
On the paps of mystic lore.
May my seven candles not be quenched!
I am an invincible fortress,
I am an immovable rock,
I am a precious stone,
I am the symbol of seven treasures.
May my wealth be in hundreds,
My years in hundreds,
Each hundred after the other!

My benefits I call to me;
The grace of the Holy Spirit be upon me!
Wholeness is the Lord's.
Wholeness is Christ's.
Bless, O Lord, Your people!

5. The Lament of the Old Woman of Beare

*The Old Woman of Beare (a peninsula in south-west Cork) is essentially a
mythological figure, ancestress of races and builder of mountains. In the eighth
and ninth centuries she is treated as an old woman who survives alone, like
Ossian after the Fianna, to take the nun's veil from Saint Cummaine the Tall,
whom we meet in No. 8 below. Hence, she is made to look back from her convent
upon a lively convivial life in the following celebrated poem. In stanza 2a her
name is given as* Buí, *which is also the name of Dursey Island. In modern Irish
she is called* Cailleach Bhéara. *I select twenty from the total of thirty-five
stanzas.*

Ebb-tide to me unlike the sea's,
Old age makes me sallow,
Although at this I may complain,
Happily floods the tide again.

I am Buí, the Old Woman of Beare,
The smock I wore was always new,
Today my means are so scant
Not even a cast-off smock could I wear.

It is riches,
Not people ye love,

sinni, ind inbaid marsaimme
batar doíni carsaimme ...

Carpait lúaith
ocus eich no beirtis búaid,
ro boí, denus, tuile díb;
bennacht for ríg roda-úaid.

Tocair mo chorp cona chré
dochum adba dír aithgni;
Tan bas mithig la Mac nDé
do-té do brith a aithni.

Ot é cnámacha cáela
ó do-éctar mo láma; –
ba hinmainiu, tan, gnítis:
bítis im ríga rána.

Ó do-éctar mo láma
ot é cnámacha cáela,
nídat fiú turcbáil, taccu,
súas tarsna maccu cáema.

It fáilti na ingena
ó thic dóib co Beltaine;
is deithbiriu damsa brón:
sech am tróg, am sentainne.

Ní feraim cobra milis;
ní marbtar muilt dom bainis;
is bec, is líath mo thrilis;
ní líach drochcaille tarais.

Ní olc lim
ce beith caille finn form chinn;
boí mór meither cech datha
form chinn oc ól daglatha.

Ním-gaib format fri nach sen
inge nammá fri Feimen:
meisse, ro miult forbuid sin;
buide beus barr Feimin.

What we loved in our day
Was people ...

Swift chariots and steeds
That carried all before them,
For a time there was a flood of these,
A blessing on the king who bestowed them!

My body of clay seeks to go
To a dwelling which it's proper to know;
When the Son of God deems it time,
Let Him come to carry off his deposit.[1]

When my arms are seen,
All bony and thin,
– Most lovingly they acted once:
Embracing glorious kings.

When my arms are seen,
All bony and thin,
– They are not worth raising, I declare,
Up over comely boys.

The girls are full of glee
When they reach May Day,
Grief is more fitting for me,
I am not only wretched but old.

No honied words do I say,
No wethers are killed for my wedding feast,
My hair is scanty and grey,
A mean veil over it will cause no regret.

It does not cause me pain
To have on my head a white veil,
Many coverings of every shade
Were on my head as we drank good ale.

I envy no one old
Except only Femen (the Tipperary Plain),
While I have worn an old person's garb,
Femen's crop is still yellow.

Lia na Ríg hi Femun,
Cathair Rónáin hi mBregun,
cían ó ros-siachtsat sína,
a lleicne nít senchrína.

Is labar tonn mora máir;
ros-gab in gaim cumgabáil;
fer maith, mac moga, in-díu
ní freiscim do chéilidiu.

Sam oíted i rrabamar
do-miult cona fhagamur;
gaim aís báides cech nduine,
domm-ánaic a fhochmuine.

Ro miult m'oítid ar thuus;
is buide lem ro-ngleus:
cid becc mo léim dar duae,
ní ba nuae in brat beus.

A-minecán! mórúar dam;
cech dercu is erchraide;
íar feis fri caindlib sorchuib
bith i ndorchuib derthaige!

Rom-boí denus la ríga
oc ól meda ocus fhína;
in-díu ibim medcuisce
eter sentainni crína.

Tonn tuili
ocus ind í aithbi áin:
a ndo-beir tonn tuili dait
beirid tonn aithbi as do láim.

Tonn tuili
ocus ind aile aithbi:
dom-áncatarsa uili
conda éolach a n-aithgni.

Céin mair insi mora máir:
dosn-ic tuile íarna tráig;

The Stone of the Kings in Femen,
The Fortress of Rónán in Bregun,[2]
Storms have long since reached them,
But their cheeks are not old and withered.

The wave of the great sea is loud,
Winter has started to raise it,
Today neither noble nor slave
Do I expect on a visit.

Summer of youth that I knew
I have spent together with its autumn,
Winter of age which submerges all men,
– To me have come its early days.

I wasted my youth to begin with,
And happy I am that I did so.
Though my leaping o'er ramparts were little,
My cloak would not have stayed new.

Very cold I am, indeed!
Every acorn must decay!
After feasting by bright candles,
To be in the darkness of an oak-church!

I've had my day with kings
Drinking mead and wine,
Whey-water now I drink
Among old shrivelled crones.

Wave of the flood,
And wave of the swift ebbing sea:
What the wave brings you at the flood
The ebb-wave takes as it recedes.

Wave of the flood
And wave of the ebbing sea:
Both of them I know,
for both have come to me.

Happy the island of the great sea:
Flood comes to it after its ebb;

os mé, ní frescu dom-í
tuile tar éisi n-aithbi.

6. Slán Seiss, A Brigit Co mBúaid

Slán seiss, a Brigit co mbúaid,
 for grúaid Lifi lir co tráig;
is tú banfhlaith buidnib slúaig
 fil for clannaib Cathaír Máir …

Ba rí Loegaire co ler,
 Ailill Áne, adbol cor;
mairid Currech cona lí
 ní mair nach rí ro boí for …

Ailend aurdairc, álaind fiss,
 fil mór flaithe fo a cniuss;
ba móu foscnad tan ad-chess
 Crimthan Coscrach ina criuss.

Gáir a ilaig iar cach mbúaid
 im chúail claideb, comtaig drend;
bríg a fían fri indna gorm,
 gloim a corn for cétaib cend.

Glés a hindéon cotad cúar,
 clúas a dúan di thengthaib bard,

As for me, I do not expect
Flood after ebb to come to me.

1. The deposit is her soul in the state of grace.
2. Bregun is in Femun, the Tipperary Plain.

6. Victorious Brigit I

*In the fifth or sixth century, Saint Brigit, 'the prophetess of Christ, the Queen
of the South, the Mary of the Gael', founded a monastery of monks and nuns
at Kildare which became the principal Church in Leinster. In a poem of 26
stanzas from the Old Irish period the flourishing state of Brigit's foundation
at Kildare is contrasted with the deserted state of Liffey-side, including the
Curragh and the Hill of Alenn (Knockawlin) where a succession of great kings
once lived in regal splendour and sought triumph in a transitory world. The
great kings of the Laigin or Leinstermen from Cathaír Már through Loegaire
Lorc, Ailill Áne and Crimthann are now of far less account than Brigit. I select
11 stanzas.*

Sit safely, victorious Brigit,
    Upon Liffey-side to the ebbing sea!
You are the princess with banded hosts
    That rules great Cathaír's family …

Leary was king to the sea,
    Ailill Áne – a mighty fate!
The Curragh in splendour endures,
    No king that has ruled it remains …

Far-famed Alenn! Splendid tidings!
    Many a prince lies under its sward;
It was greater than could be told
    When conquering Crimthann was seen in its bosom.

The cry of triumph after each victory
    Round massed swords in solid strength,
The might of its troops against the dark-blue battle line,
    The sound of its horns above hundreds of heads.

The ring of its very active bent anvils,
    The sound of songs heard there from the tongues of bards,

47

bruth a fer fri comlann nglan,
    cruth a ban fri hoenach n-ard.

A ól meda for cach mbruig,
    a graig allmar, ilar túath,
a seinm rond di rigaib fer
    fo duilnib sleg cóicrind crúach.

A céoil binni i cach thráth,
    a fínbarc for tonngur flann,
a fross argait ordain móir,
    a tuirc óir a tírib Gall...

Foglas a ngen tibes duitt
    a maig réid túaith Críchaib Cuirc,
di cach lín ron alt a úair
    do-rigni lúaith Life Luirc.

Currech Lifi lir co hor,
    Currech Sétnai, síth co ler,
is mór ríg fris-rala cor
    Currech Corpri Niöd Fer...

A Brigit 'sa tír ad-chíu,
    is cách a úair immud-rá,
ro gab do chlú for a chlú
    ind ríg, is tú forda-tá.

Táthut bithfhlaith lasin Ríg
    cen a tír i fil do rúaim;
a uë Bresail maic Déin,
    slán seiss, a Brigit co mbúaid.

The ardour of its men at the glorious contest,
   The beauty of its women at the high assembly.

Drinking of mead there in every mansion,
   Its noble steeds, its many tribes,
The jingling of chains on the wrists of men
   Under blades of bloody five-edged spears.

Sweet melodies there at every hour,
   Its wine-barque upon the purple flood,
its shower of silver of great splendour,
   Its torques of gold from the lands of the Gaul...

Bright is the smile that smiles at you
   From the plain north of the lands of Corc,
Of each generation it reared in turn
   The Liffey of Lorc has made dust.

The Curragh of Liffey to ocean's edge,
   The Curragh of Sétna at peace to the sea,
The Curragh of Cairpre Nia Fer
   Has brought many kings to their knees...

O Brigit whose land I behold,
   On which each in turn has moved around,
Your fame has outshone the fame of the king,
   – It's you that are over them all.

You have everlasting rule with the King,
   Apart from the land where you lie buried;
Grandchild of Bresal, son of Dian,
   Sit safely, victorious Brigit!

7. Brigit Buadach

Brigit búadach,
Búaid na fine,
Siur Ríg nime,
Nár in duine,
Eslind luige,
 Lethan breo.
Ro-siacht noíbnem
Mumme Goídel,
Riar na n-oíged,
Oíbel ecnai,
Ingen Dubthaig,
Duine úallach,
Brigit búadach,
 Bethad beo.

7. Victorious Brigit II

The epithet búadach *'victorious', often used of kings and heroes, is the one commonly applied to Brigit. See Poem No. 6 and Introduction, p. 13. A national saint in her own right, Brigit has been somewhat overshadowed by Patrick, but the variants of her name current for Irish girls are in themselves evidence of her enduring importance: compare the forms* Brigid, Breege, Breda, Breed, Bride, Bridie, *beside the diminutive in* −een. *Behind the Christian saint of the hagiographers and the accounts of wonders curiously performed, and behind the oral and literary traditions, one can spy the figure of a pre-Christian goddess.*[1] *Brigit is represented in the early poetry as Mother of Christ and equal in rank to Mary, and as 'The Mary of the Gael'. Hence the tradition of Brigit goes deeper as well as further back than that of the Briton, Patrick.*

Victorious Brigit,
Glory of kindred,
Heaven-King's sister,
Noble person,
Perilous oath,[2]
   Far-flung flame.
She has reached holy Heaven,
Gaeldom's foster-mother,
Support of strangers,
Spark of wisdom,
Daughter of Dubthach,
High-minded lady,
Victorious Brigit,
   The living one of life.

1. See Introduction p. 13.
2. I.e. Dangerous to swear by – for perjurers.

8. Comrac Líadaine Ocus Cuirithir

I

A tech mór
fo-longat na tuireda,
dia mbeith nech no-dálad dáil,
timnae dáib co fuineda.

Nech don-ísed ba mithig
a topor file fiad tig,
ferait a lúadain imbi,
uissi áilli imrinni.

Ro-lá temel dom roscaib,
am dillig ar inchoscaib,
conid Líadain con-gairiu
cach banscál nád athgniniu.

A ben cosind remorchois,
ní fúar do shét di márchlois,
nícon festor fo chailliu
banscál badid cíallaidiu:

Mac in míl
anas adaig fo linnib,

8. Líadan and Cuirithir

The love of Líadan and Cuirithir is one of the great romantic stories of early Ireland. It is extant in a ninth century Old Irish form as a string of poems threaded upon a tenuous narrative which leaves much to the imagination.

Both Líadan and Cuirithir were poets, she from Corca Dhuibhne in west Kerry and he from Connacht. They met in Connacht where she was on a professional tour, and they made a tryst for the following year at her home in Kerry on the understanding that she would then consort with him. By the time he arrived there she had taken the veil.

I. Trysting

When Cuirithir arrived at Líadan's village, he met the so-called óinmit *or 'Fool', Mac Da Cherda, who was also chief poet of Ireland.*[1] *After some parleying, Mac Da Cherda agreed to go into the Court, and 'using his own wits' to convey to 'the tall woman' (Líadan, now a nun) that Cuirithir wished to meet her at the well. The narrative continues:* He went into the house. She was there in her bedroom with four other women. He sat down, but no notice was taken of him. Then he said:

> O manor house
> Which the pillars support,
> If any there be who have made a tryst,
> The assignation for them is till sunset.
>
> It were time that one should visit
> The well in front of the house,
> Beautiful, tapering larks
> Wing their way round it.
>
> Darkness has fallen on my eyes,
> I can make out no signs,
> So Líadan[2] is what I call
> Every woman I do not know.
>
> O woman with the firm foot,
> Your like for great fame I have not found,
> Beneath nun's veil will not be known
> A woman more discerning:
>
> The son of the creature
> That stays under pools at night

fo-longat cot idnaidiu
cossa glassa fo rinnib.

II

Líadan:

Carsam, ním ráinic a less,
Cuirithir int athéces;
inmain fíada da coss nglass
bid dirsan a bithingnas.

In lecc fri derthach an-dess
forsa mbíd int athéces,
meinic tíagar di im cach ndé
fescor iar mbuaid ernaigde.

Nícon bia aice bó
ná dairti ná dartado,
nícon bia cnáim do leiss
for láim deiss ind athécis.

Cuirithir:

Inmain guthán ro-cluiniur,
fáilte fris nícon-lamur,
acht is ed at-biur nammá:
is inmain in guthán sa.

Líadan:

Guth dom-adbat tria cletha
is maith dó dom-increcha,
is ed do-gní frimm in guth:
nachom-léci do chotlud.

Awaits thee
On peaked grey feet upright.[3]

II. In the Monastery

Then she went off with him for a time and on their return they placed themselves under the spiritual guidance of the famous Cummaine the Tall, a seventh century saint associated chiefly with West Munster.

As confessor or 'soul friend' (anmchara), Cummaine imposed a restriction upon them; they were free to talk to but not to look at each other. So when either visited the tombs of the saints, the other's cell would be closed.

Then Líadan said:

> Cuirithir, once a poet
> Loved me; I had no good of it;
> Dear the lord of the two grey feet,[4]
> It will be sad to be without him for ever.

> The flagstone south of the oak church
> Where the one-time poet used to be,
> 'Tis there I often go each day
> At eve after the triumph of prayer.

> Never will he have a cow
> Or young heifers or bulls,
> Never will a thighbone lie
> On the one-time poet's right side.

Cuirithir: Dear the little voice I hear,
   I dare not bid it welcome,
   But this only do I say:
   This little voice is dear.

Líadan: The voice that comes to me through the wattled
   stakes rightly incriminates me,
   What the voice does to me is this:
   It will not let me sleep.

'Foid far ndís innocht,' ar Cummaine, 'ocus téit léignid becc etraib, co ná dernaid anespa.'

Is and as-bert som:

> Másu óenadaig at-bir
> fesi dam-sae la Líadain,
> méti la laech nod-fiad
> ind adaig ní archriad.

Is and as-bert Líadain:

> Másu óenadaig at-bir
> feis dam-sae la Cuirithir,
> cid blíadain do-bérmais fris,
> baíthium imma-rordamais.

IV

Luidsium didiu co mboí i Cill Letrech i tír na nDéise ina ailithri. Do-luidsi for a iarairsium et dixit:

> Cen áinius
> in gním hí do-rigénus:
> an ro charus ro cráidius.

> Ba mire
> nad dernad a airersom
> mainbed omun Ríg nime.

> Nibu amlos
> dosom in dul dúthracair,
> ascnam sech phéin i Pardos.

III. Chastity Test

Now Líadan begins to chafe against Cummaine's restrictive attitude, so he allows them a dangerous freedom:

'Sleep by each other tonight,' said Cummaine 'and let a little scholar lie between you, lest you do anything unseemly.'

Then Cuirithir said:

> If it is one night you say
> I am to sleep with Líadan,
> Much would it weigh with the layman who'd sleep
> That the night did not fade away.

Then Líadan said:

> If it is one night you say
> I am to sleep with Cuirithir,
> Though we should spend a year at it,
> I should still have matter for converse.

IV. Parting

The experiment appears to have failed and Cummaine decided to banish Cuirithir. The narrative continues:

He went on pilgrimage to Cill Letrech in the land of the Déisi in Waterford, where he probably became a monk. *She came seeking him and said:*

> Unpleasing
> The deed I have done:
> The one I loved I have grieved.

> 'Twere madness
> Were his wish unachieved,
> But for dread of Heaven's King.

> Not unavailing
> To him the way that he chose:
> Faring without pain to Paradise.

Bec mbríge
ro chráidi frimm Cuirithir;
frissium ba mór mo míne.

Mé Líadan;
ro carussa Cuirithir;
is fírithir ad-fíadar.

Gair bása
i comaitecht Chuirithir;
frissium ba maith mo gnássa.

Céol caille
fom-chanad la Cuirithir,
la fogur fairrge flainne.

Do-ménainn
ní cráidfed frimm Cuirithir
do dálaib cacha dénainn.

Ní chela:
ba hésium mo chridesherc,
cia no carainn cách chena.

Deilm ndega
ro thethainn mo chridese;
ro-fess, nicon bía cena.

Is é, didiu, crád do-ratsi fairsium a lúas ro gab caille. Amail ron-
cúalasom a tuidechtsi aniar, luidsom hi curuch forsan fairci, co ndechaid
inna ailithriu, co ná accasi hinnunn. 'Do-cóidsom a fecht so,' olsi.
    Ind lecc fora-mbídsom ac ernaigthe, ro boí sí for inn leicc sin co n-
erbailtsi.

A trifling thing
That displeased Cuirithir with me,
To him I was gentle and mild.

I am Líadan;
I loved Cuirithir;
It is as true as they say.

Brief the spell
That I was with Cuirithir;
Sweet was my intimacy with him.

Forest music
Sang to me beside Cuirithir,
With the voice of the wild sea.

I had believed
I would not have vexed Cuirithir
By any act or deed.

Hide it not!
He was my heart's desire –
If I loved the world beside.

A surge of fire
Has split my heart.
- Without him it will never survive.

*Now the way she had wrung his heart was her haste in taking the veil.
When he heard that she was coming from the west, he set out in a curragh
on the sea and took to strange lands and pilgrimage, so that she never
saw him more. 'This time he has gone' she said.*

The flagstone on which he used to pray, she was upon it till she died.

1. The *óinmit* was a rather mysterious figure. He could combine contraries and
be either a simpleton inspired, half-witted but shrewd, a professional jester, or
an entertainer. Mac Da Cherda, well-known in the tradition is described as 'a
man full of understanding and of the grace of the Holy Spirit.' Later sources
represent him as half-brother to the saint, Cummaine the Tall, who enters our
story in the next section.
2. As if *Líadan* were from *Líath-án* 'Grey Lady'.
3. Cuirithir's surname is *mac Doborchon* 'Son of the Otter'.
4. In stanza lc Cuirithir is described as the otter in human form, with two grey
feet. In stanza 3ab, cow, heifers and bulls represent wife and children by a
familiar pastoral image. See Introduction p. 9.

9. Bennacht Fort

At-rubairt Daniél ua Liathaiti, airchinnech Lis Móir, ocá guide don mnaí. Esseom ropo anmchara disi. Baí-si immurgu ocá thothlugud-som. Is and as-bert-som:

A ben, bennacht fort – ná ráid!
  Imráidem dáil mbrátha buain!
A-tá irchra for cach ndúil:
  Ad-águr dul i n-úir n-uair.

Im-ráidi baís cen bríg mbaí:
  Is suaichnid ní gaís fris-ngní.
A n-as-bir-siu bid rád fás:
  Bid nessa ar mbás 'síu 'ma-rrí.

A n-airchenn fil ar ar cinn
  Bad mebor linn (éirim ngann):
Sunn cia no cráidem in Ríg,
  Batin aithrig is tír thall.

Ríched ní renaim ar chol;
  Dam ad-fíther cía do-gner.
Ní nad faigbe-siu iar sin
  Ní thaibre ar bin, a ben.

Léic uait a n-í 'condat fhil,
  Do chuit i nnim náchas ren;
For fóesam nDé eirg dot tig,
  Bennacht uaim-se beir, a ben!

Messe tussu, tussu mé,
  Águr, áig dé Fiada fó!
Guid-siu, gigsea Coimdid cáid!
  A ben, ná ráid ní bas mó.

Ná bí for seilg neich nád maith
  Dáig not chuirfe in Fhlaith for cel;
Áig-siu, águr Críst cen chin!
  Ná ro-lámur tríst, a ben!

9. A Blessing on Thee

Daniel Ó Liathaite, abbot of Lismore,[1] spoke these verses when a woman was entreating him. He was her confessor, but she was soliciting him. Then he said:

O woman, a blessing on you! Do not speak!
　　Let us think of the court of eternal judgment!
Decay is the fate of every creature;
　　　　– I fear going into cold clay.

What you contemplate is bootless folly;
　　'Tis clearly not wisdom that you serve.
What you say will be empty words,
　　　　– Our death will be nearer before it comes to pass.

The fated end that awaits us
　　Let us remember! A short journey!
If here we aggrieve the King,
　　　　We will rue it in the land yonder.

I sell not Heaven for sin;
　　If I do, I'll be repaid.
What you will not get afterwards
　　　　Give not for evil, O woman!

Abandon that which you're about,
　　Your share in Heaven do not sell,
In God's safeguard go to your house,
　　　　Take a blessing from me, O woman!

I and you, you and I –
　　Let me dread, dread you the day of the good God;
Pray you, I shall pray the holy Lord,
　　　　O woman, say no more!

Pursue not that which is not good,
　　For it will lose you the Kingdom;
Fear you, let me fear sinless Christ!
　　　　Let me not risk malediction, woman!

'Bid fír ón,' or sisi. Ro shlécht si for a bith-denma-som in eret ro
boí i mbethaid.

10. Fingal Rónáin

Rónán: Is úar gaeth
i ndorus tige na llaech;
batar inmaine laích
bítis etrainn ocus gaíth.

Cotail, a ingen Echach,
is mór aichre na gaíthe;
saeth limmsa Mael Fhothartaig
do guin i cin mná baíthe.

Cotail, a ingen Echach;
ní sám lim, cen co tola
aicsin Maíle Fothartaig
inna léini lán fola.

Ise: Monúar, a marbáin chúile
immon-rúalaid mór súile,
a ndo-ringénsam di chul
rop sí do phían iar t'athchur.

Eisean: Cotail, a ingen Echach,
nídat mera na doíni;
cia broena-su do brattán
ní hé mo maccán choíni.

'Thus it shall be!' said she. She bowed down before his perpetual purity as long as he was alive.

1. An abbot of Lismore and Cork of this name died in AD 863; see EIL, p. 176. The poem is of the ninth century.

10. Rónán's Lament

This is from the late Old Irish saga, Fingal Rónáin. *King Rónán of Leinster, a widower, was advanced in years when he married the young daughter of King Eochaid of Dunseverick (near the Giant's Causeway on the Antrim coast). The young queen conceived a passion for Rónán's manly son, Mael Fhothartaig, whose favourite pastime was hunting with his hounds Dathlenn and Doílín. Mael Fhothartaig spurned her advances, whereupon she accused him falsely to Rónán and had him killed, with his friend Congal. Mael Fhothartaig's foster-brothers then went north to Dunseverick, lured Eochaid with his wife and son to the border, slew them and brought back their heads.*

Rónán: Cold is the wind
In the door of the warriors' house,
Beloved were the warriors
Who used to come between me and the wind.

Sleep, daughter of Eochaid,
Great is the bitterness of the wind,
Grievous to me is Mael Fhothartaig's death
Through the guilt of a wanton woman.

Sleep, daughter of Eochaid,
But even if you do not sleep,
It is no comfort to me to see Mael Fhothartaig
In his tunic covered with blood.

She: Alas, O corpse in the corner
That many eyes have passed over,
The sin that we committed
Was your suffering after your exile.[1]

He: Sleep, daughter of Eochaid,
The people are not mad:
Though you wet your cloak with tears,
It's not for my son you weep.

[The severed heads of her people are tossed to her and she kills herself.]

Rónán: Ro gab Echaid oínléini
      iar mbeith i leinn lebairthe;
  in brónán fil for Dún nÁis
    atá for Dún Sebairche.

  Tabraid biad, tabraid dig
    do choin Maíle Fothartaig,
  ocus tabrad nech aile
    biad do choin Chongaile.

  Tabraid biad, tabraid dig
    do choin Maíle Fothartaig,
  cú fir do-bérad biad
    do neoch, cid luaig no criad.

  Saeth limm cúrad Daithlinne
    flescaib tinnib tar toebu;
  ní fil ar n-aithber fuirri,
    ní sí ro rir ar coemu.

  Doíléne
  acumsa fo-roígéne;
    a cenn for choim cáich ar úair
    oc cuindchid neich nád fogéba.

  Ind fhir, ind oïc, ind eich
  bítis imm Maíl Fothartaig,
    niptis formtig caemna neich
    i mbethaid a n-airchinnig.

  Ind fhir, ind oïc, ind eich
  bítis im Maíl Fothartaig,
    do-gnítis cen cosc a-maig,
    fo-fhertais grafainn ngraigig.

  Ind fhir, ind oïc, ind eich
  bítis im Maíl Fothartaig,
    Batar meinci-som úaraib
    fo ilaig iar mbithbúadaib.

  Muinter Maíle Fothartaig
    cet limm cenptis desruithi;

Rónán: Eochaid has donned a single shirt
       After being in a long, warm mantle,
  The sorrow upon Naas
      Is also on Dunseverick.

Give food, give drink
To the hound of Mael Fhothartaig,
    And let someone else
    Give food to Congal's hound.

Give food, give drink
To the hound of Mael Fhothartaig,
    The hound of a man who would give food,
    Though he had to buy it at a price.

I grieve for the beating of Dathlenn
    With sore rods on the flanks,
With her I have no fault to find,
    It was not she who sold our dear ones.

Doílín
Has served me;
    Her head for a while in every bosom
    Seeking one she will not find.

The men, the youths, the steeds
That were about Mael Fhothartaig
    Did not envy anyone's bounty
    In the lifetime of their leader.

The men, the youths, the steeds
That were about Mael Fhothartaig
    Exercised unhindered on the plain,
    Raced their many horses.

The men, the youths, the steeds
That were about Mael Fhothartaig
    Often cried out in exultation
    After great victories.

The band of Mael Fhothartaig,
   – Though I concede they were not dishonoured –

ní maith ro gabsat oc fiur
do-icced a n-esbuithi.

Mo mac-sa Mael Fhothartaig
diambo adbae fid fota,
ní scoirtis cen immairi
ríg ná rígdamnai oca.

Mo mac-sa Mael Fhothartaig
imme-réid Albain oraig,
ba laech etar laechradaib
im-beired a baind foraib.

Mo-mac-sa Mael Fhothartaig
ba hé cuingid na cúaine,
éo finn fota for lassair
ro gab adbai co n-úairi.

11. Reicne Fothaid Canainne

Did not well stand
   By the man who made good their needs.

My son Mael Fhothartaig
   Whose home was the spacious wood,
   – Neither king nor king's son
   Would unyoke there without keeping watch.

My son Mael Fhothartaig,
   Who had ridden round gap-coasted Scotland,
Was a warrior among warriors
   and took sway over them.

My son Mael Fhothartaig
   Was champion of the pack,
Tall, slender yew ablaze
   – He has taken a cold abode.

1. Mael Fhothartaig had gone to Scotland for a time to escape her importunities.

11. Fothad Canainne's Poem
The Fatal Tryst

Fothad Canainne was one of three famous brothers all called Fothad who were leaders of roving war bands. Our Fothad operated in Connacht and was at loggerheads with the leader of a Munster war-band, Ailill Flann. As the manuscript puts it: Ba h-amru delb Fothaid ol baí Oilill, acht ba h-amru ben Oilella ocus ba h-áille oldás ben Fhothaid (Fothad's shape was more marvellous than that of Ailill, but Ailill's wife was more marvellous and delightful than Fothad's wife).

Fothad sent a messenger in secret to Ailill's wife to woo her for him. She said that she would not consider a proposal from Fothad unless he gave her her bride-price, namely, a bushel of gold, a bushel of silver, and a bushel of white bronze. Now each man of Fothad's household had six rivets in his spear, two of gold, two of silver and two of white bronze. They all then contributed one rivet of each metal, leaving a like amount in the spears. In this way the bride-price was paid. Fothad trysted with her and carried her off, with Ailill and all his forces in hot pursuit. The long-threatened encounter between these inveterate enemies then took place. Fothad fell there and was beheaded. The woman then appeared on the battlefield and Fothad's head addressed her.

The poem is probably ninth century. Of the 49 stanzas, many detailing the spoils left by Fothad on the battlefield, I select 16.

A ben nacham aicille!
ní fritt atá mo menme;
   atá mo menme co lléic
   isind immairiuc oc Féic.

Atá mo chorpán cruach
i taíb Leitrech dá mBruach;
   atá mo chenn cen nigi
   eter fíana for garbshligi.

Dochtae do neuch dáiles dáil
fácbáil dála éca fri láim;
   in dáil dálta co Clárach
   tuarnecht im robánad.

Ní mé m'oenur i mmúr thal
do-chúaid fordul i ndáil ban;
   ní ar aithbiur cid dit ágh
   is duaig ar ndedendál.

Di chéin do-roacht do dáil,
baí gráin for mo choicni máir;
   ma ro-fesmais bid am-ne
   ba assa ní tairiste.

Ním rumartsa m'amusrad,
fían gormainech goburglas;
   a techt i n-úire adbai
   dirsan dond éochaill amrai.

Co a tiugdáil batar lúaith,
ad-cosnaitis bidbad búaid,
   fo-cantais rainn, trom a ngáir,
   cinsit di chlainn ruirech ráin.

Ba é fíanlach seng subach
Cosin aimsir i rrubad;
   arus-foet caill duileglas
   ropo coicne uilemnas…

Ná tuinite aidche úath
i lleirg eter lechta cúan;

Woman, do not speak to me,
My mind is not on you;
   My mind is still upon
   The encounter at Féic.[1]

My bloody corpse lies
At the side of Leitir Dá mBruach;
   Unwashed lies my head
   Between warrior-bands in fierce slaughter.

'Tis short-sighted for one who makes a tryst
To cast the tryst with death aside;
   The tryst that was made for Clara,
   – I have come to it in deathly pallor.

I'm not the only one to go astray
On woman-tryst in passion's blaze,
   No reproach to you, though 'twas on your account,
   Our last tryst is wretched.

From afar I came to meet you,
It appalled my noble company.
   Had we but known it would be thus,
   It would have been easy not to persist.

My band of noble-faced, grey-horsed warriors
Did not betray me.
   Alas for the splendid yew forest,
   That they should go into a house of clay!

They were swift to their final tryst,
Ever they sought victory over the foe,
   They would sing a song, deep was their voice,
   They were of noble, princely stock.

They were a merry, lithe-limbed band
Until the moment they were slain,
   The green-leaved forest received them,
   A most warlike band of men...

Do not await the terror of night
Among the graves of the hosts on the battlefield;

ní fíu cobra fri fer marb;
fot-ruim dot daim, beir latt m'fhadb.

Is dúal deitsi, sét nach lac,
m'fhidchell, ata-rella lat,
    bruinnid fuil shoer for a bil,
    ní cían di shunn indas-fil.

Is mór colnae cúan rinnech
san chan imma deirginnech,
    dosn-eim dos dlúith dairbri rúaid
    i taíb ind fhirt aniar-túaid.

Ataat immunn san chan
mór fodb asa forderg bal;
    dremun inathor dímar
    nodus nig an Morrígan.

Don-árlaid, dobail oígi,
is sí cotan-assoídi;
    is mór di fhodbaib niges
    dremun in caisgen tibes.

Ro lá a moing tar a ais;
cride im aithrecht noda ais;
    cid gar di shunn úann i mbé
    ná fubthad úaman do gné.

Scarfaid frit céin mo chorp toll,
m'anam do phianad la Donn;
    serc betho cé is mire
    inge adrad Ríg nime.

Is é in lon teimen tibes
imchomarc cáich bes ires;
    síabra mo chobra, mo gné,
    a ben, nacham aicille.

You should not speak to a dead man,
Go home and take my spoils with you.

Yours is my chessboard, no mean treasure,
Take it with you;
    Noble blood drips on its rim,
    Not far from here it's lying.

Many a corpse of the hosts of spearmen
Lies here and there around its crimson woof,
    A dense red oak bush hides it
    By the side of the mound to the north-west.

Here and there around us are
Many a blood-red spoil,
    Horrid the huge entrails
    Which the Morrígu[2] washes.

She has come to us, an ominous guest,
'Tis she that incited our contest,
    Many are the spoils she washes,
    Dreadful her twisted smile of hate.

Backwards she has tossed her mane
– My heart in my former shape fears her;
    Though she is close to you here,
    Let not fear assail you!

My riddled body will part from you a while,
My soul will go to its torment with Donn,[3]
    Save for the worship of Heaven's King
    Earthly love is folly.

'Tis the dark blackbird that laughs
A greeting to all believers;
    Spectral my speech, my face,
    Woman, do not speak to me!

1. Féic = Linn Féic (Fiacc's Pool) in the river Boyne near Slane.
2. A war goddess.
3. Donn, Lord of the Dead in Gaelic mythology, was located at Tech Duinn, on
an island off the Kerry coast.

12. It É Saigte Gona Súain

Créda ingen Guairiu ru chan na runnusa de Dínertach, mac
Gúairi maic Nechtain do Uib Fidgenti. Di-connuircsi isin treus
Aidne ro geghin secht ngoine deac for seglach a léniod. Ro-
carostoirsie ierum. Is ann is-pertsie:

It é saigte gona súain
cech thrátha i n-aidchi adúair
serccoí, lia gnása, íar ndé,
fir a tóeb thíre Roigne.

Rográd fir ala thíre
ro-shíacht sech a chomdíne
ruc mo lí (ni lór do dath);
ním-léci do thindabrad.

Binniu laídib a labrad
acht Ríg nime nóebadrad:
án bréo cen bréthir mbraise,
céle tana tóebthaise.

Imsa naídiu robsa nár:
ní biinn fri dul dodál;
ó do-lod i n-inderb n-aís
rom-gab mo théte togaís.

Táthum cech maith la Gúaire,
la ríg nAidni adúaire;
tocair mo menma óm thúathaib
isin íath i nIrlúachair.

Canair i n-íath Aidni áin
im thóebu Cille Colmáin,
án bréo des Luimnech lechtach
díanid comainm Dínertach.

Cráidid mo chride cainech,
a Chríst cáid, a fhoraided:
it é saigte gona súain
cech thrátha i n-aidchi adúair.

12. Créd's Lament

Créd, daughter of Guaire, sang these quatrains for Dínertach, son of Guaire, son of Nechtan of the Uí Fhidgente. She had seen him in the battle of Aidne[1] pierced seventeen times through the breast of his tunic. She loved him after that. It is then she said:

The arrows that murder sleep
At every hour in the bitter-cold night:
Love's lament for time spent at twilight
With a man from the land of Roigne.

Great love for one from another land
Who excelled those of his day
Has taken my bloom; little colour is left;
It does not let me sleep.

His speech was sweeter then all songs
Save pious adoration of Heaven's King;
Bright flame with no word of boasting,
A slender, soft-sided mate.

As a child I was modest,
I was not one for amorous trysting;
Since I reached the uncertain age,
My wantonness has beguiled me.

I have everything good with Guaire,
King of cold Aidne;
But my mind seeks to go from my people
To the land of Irluachair.

In the glorious land of Aidne,
Around the sides of Cell Cholmáin
Men sing of the bright flame from the south of Limerick
Of the graves, whose name is Dínertach.

His grievous death, O chaste Christ,
Wrings my tender heart.
These are the arrows that murder sleep
At every hour in the bitter-cold night.

1. Or Carn Conaill, fought in AD 649 between King Guaire of South Galway and Diarmait, King of Ireland, the victor. The poem was composed about AD 800.

13. Tecosca Cormaic

'A huí Chuind, a Chormaic' (ol Cairpre)
'Cia etargén mná?'
'Ní hansa'(ol Cormac):
'Nosn-etargén ocus nísn-etargléim:
Feidle miscne,   5
dermatcha seirce,
ítfaide toile,
deithide cairddine,
cundamna écnaig,
écundla airechta,   10
airrechtga ugrai,
étairise rúne,
rudracha taíthe,
gárechtga éoit...

fanna immargaile,   15
inire debtha,
díairithe lítha,
bróncha cuirmthige...
todiúre ciúil,
étradcha lige,   20
labra écundla,
tuillmecha augrai,
cessachtaige biid...

béoda tingill,
tomtencha uilc,   25
santacha dála,
duabaise tairirid,
tromda coblige,
bodra forcetail,
dalla dagairle,   30
dochéille sochaide,

13. The Instructions of Cormac

The 'Instructions of Cormac' (Tecosca Cormaic) is the title of one of the collections of proverbial or wise sayings which come down to us from the Old Irish period, that is, before AD 900. They are in the guise of instructions to the prince, Cairbre Lifeachair, from his royal father, Cormac mac Airt. They include a long anti-feminist passage which shows how the bias against women had developed in medieval times. From this we print a short selection.

'O Cormac, grandson of Conn' (said Cairbre)
'How do you understand women?'
'Not difficult' (said Cormac):
'I understand them – and I make no distinction between them:
They are steadfast in hate,   5
Forgetful in love,
Thirsting for lust,
Anxious for friendship,
Accustomed to slander,
Indiscreet in an assembly,   10
Aggressive in a quarrel,
Not to be trusted with a secret,
Persistent in pilfering,
Loud in their jealousy...

Feeble in a contest,   15
Malicious in strife,
Noisy at a feast,
Sorrowful in an ale-house...
Tearful during music,
Lustful in bed,   20
Irresponsible in speech,
Fomentors of strife,
Grudging with food...

Quick to promise,
Meditating evil,   25
Eager for company,
Gloomy on a journey,
Troublesome bed-fellows,
Deaf to instruction,
Blind to good counsel,   30
Fatuous in society,

míancha blassachta,
mina tairberta...

canait nád comaillit,
triallait nád forbait,   35
for-comat nád comraicet,
ro-íallat nád astat,
ad-gellat nád fírat,
do-rairngerat nád chomallat,
con-rannat nád fúaslaigit,   40
ro-collet nád íccat
for-fhodlat nád tinólat,
ro-nertat nád dernat...

ferr a flescad a fóenblegon,
ferr a sroigled a subugud,   45
ferr a túargain a táltugud
ferr a mbúalad a mbuidechas,
ferr a foimtiu a tairisi,
ferr a tróethad a turgorud,
ferr a ndinge a ngrádugud...   50

At tonna not-báidet,
at tene not-loisc,
at airm défháebracha not-chloidmet,
at legaim ar lenamain,
at nathracha ar túaichli,   55
at dorcha i soillsi,
at olca etir maithi,
at messa etir olcu.

14. Trecheng Breth Féni

1. Trí coíl ata ferr fo-longat in mbith: coíl srithite hi folldeirb,
coíl foichne for tuinn, coíl snáithe dar dorn degmná.

2. Trí aithgine in domuin: brú mná, uth bó, ness gobann.

76

Longing for titbits,
Stingy with gifts...

They announce what they do not perform,
They attempt what they do not finish,   35
They retain what they do not acquire,
They attach what they do not legally secure,
They make vows that they do not keep,
They promise what they do not carry out,
They share what they do not redeem,   40
They destroy what they do not pay for.
They scatter what they do not gather,
They confirm what they cannot accomplish...

Better to whip them than to humour them,
Better to scourge them than to gladden them,   45
Better to smite them than to coddle them,
Better to beat them than to please them,
Better to beware of them than to trust them,
Better to subdue them than to fondle them,
Better to crush them than to cherish them...   50

They are waves that drown you,
They are fire that burns you,
They are two-edged weapons that cut you,
They are leeches for clinging,
They are serpents for cunning,   55
They are darkness in light,
They are bad among the good,
They are worse among the bad.

14: The Triads of Ireland
(Late Ninth Century)

1. Three slenders that best sustain the world: the slender
   stream of milk from the cow's teat into the pail; the slender
   blade of green corn upon the ground; the slender thread over
   the hand of a skilled woman.
2. Three renewals of the world: a woman's womb; a cow's udder;
   a smith's moulding block.

3. Trí duirn ata dech for bith: dorn degshaír, dorn degmná, dorn deggobann.

4. Trí bainne cétmuintire: bainne fola, bainne dér, bainne aillse.

5. Trí banlae: Lúan, Mairt, Cétaín. Mná co firu indib, bid mó a serc la firu indá serc a fer leo-som ocus beit a mná tar éis na fer sin.

6. Trí ferlae: Dardaín, Aíne, Domnach. Mná co firu indib, beitit na mná sin fo dígrád ocus beitit a fir dia n-éisi. Satharn immorro, is laithe coitchenn. Is comlíth dóib. Lúan sáer do dul fri cach les.

7. a) Trí luchra ata messa: luchra tuinde, luchra mná baíthe, luchra con foléimnige.
   b) Trí gena ata messu brón: gen snechta oc legad, gen do mná frit íar mbith fhir aili lé, gen chon fhoilmnich.

8. Trí dorchae ná dlegat mná do imthecht: Dorcha cíach, dorcha aidche, dorcha feda.

9. Trí búada téiti: Ben cháemh, ech maith, cú luath.

10. Trí fuchachta nad increnat slabrai: A gabáil ar écin, a sleith tri mescai, a turtugud do ríg.

11. Trí mná ná dlegat díri: Ben lasma cuma cipé las foí, ben gatach, ben aupthach.

12. Trí maic nad rannat orbai: Mac muini ocus aurlai ocus ingine fo thrilis.

13. Trí noíll do ná dlegar frithnoíll: Noíll mná fri húaitni, noíll fir mairb, noíll díthir.

3. Three hands that are best in the world: the hand of a good carpenter; the hand of a skilled woman; the hand of a good smith.
4. Three drops of a wedded wife: a drop of blood; a teardrop; a drop of sweat.
5. Three woman-days: Monday, Tuesday, Wednesday. If women go to men on those days, the men will love them better than they the men, and the women will survive the men.
6. Three man-days: Thursday, Friday, Sunday. Women who go to men on those days will not be loved, and their husbands will survive them. Saturday, however, is a common day. It is equally lucky for them. Monday is a free day to undertake any business.
7. a) Three worst smiles: the smile of the wave; the smile of a wanton woman; the grin of the dog about to leap at you.
   b) Three smiles that are worse than sorrow: the smile of melting snow; the smile of your wife at you after another man has been with her; the grin of a hound about to leap at you.
8. Three darknesses women should not enter: the darkness of mist; the darkness of night; the darkness of a wood.

9. Three glories of a gathering: a beautiful wife, a good horse, a swift hound.
10. Three cohabitations that do not pay a marriage portion: taking her by force; outraging her by stealth through drunkenness; her violation by a king.
11. Three women who are not entitled to honour-price: a woman who cares not with whom she sleeps; a thief; a sorceress.

12. Three sons that do not share inheritance: a son begotten in a thicket; the son of a slave; the son of a girl still in tresses.

13. Three oaths that do not require a counter-oath: the oath of a woman in birth-pangs; the oath of a dead man; the oath of a landless man.

15. Mé Éba

Mé Éba, ben Ádaim uill;
mé ro sháraig Ísu thall;
mé ro thall nem ar mo chloinn:
cóir is mé do-chóid sa crann.

Ropa lem rígtheg dom réir;
olc in míthoga rom-thár;
olc in cosc cinad rom-chrín:
forír! ní hidan mo lám.

Mé tuc in n-uball anúas
do-chúaid tar cumang mo chraís;
in céin marat-sam re lá
de ní scarat mná re baís.

Ní bíad eigred in cach dú;
ní bíad geimred gáethmar glé,
ní bíad iffern, ní bíad brón,
ní bíad oman, minbad mé.

16. Ciodh Ma nDeilighe

Ben: Ciodh ma ndeilighe
Mo mhac grádhach riom?
Toradh mo bhronn,
mé ro thuisimh,

80

15. I am Eve

This eleventh century poem offers the traditional view of the first woman; see Introduction, page 15.

I am Eve, great Adam's wife,
I that outraged Jesus of old,
From my children Heaven I stole,
By right 'tis I should have gone on the Tree.

My house was royal, to my will;
Ill the evil choice that brought me low;
Ill the wicked counsel that withered me;
Alas! My hand is not clean.

I that plucked the apple
Which went down my narrow gullet;
For that, all the days of their lives
Women will not cease from folly.

In no place would there be ice,
And no glistening windy winter,
There would be no hell nor sorrow,
And no terror, but for me.

16: Why Do You Part Me?
Massacre of the Innocents

The babes who were slaughtered in lieu of the infant Jesus are brought to dramatic life in this unusual and striking composition which is reminiscent of the early rudimentary biblical drama. It is taken from a late Middle Irish homiletic romance on the subject of Christ's childhood.

Then, as the executioner tore her son from her breast, one of the women said:

Why do you part me
From my darling son?
Fruit of my womb,
It was I brought him forth;

mo chích ro ibh,
mo bhrú ros iomarchar,
m'inne ro shúigh,
mo chridhe ro shás,
mo bheatha rob é,
mo bhás a bhreith uaim;
mo neart ro thráigh,
m'innsce ro shocht,
mo shúile ro dhall.

Ben Aile: Mo mhac bheire uaim,
ní hé do-ní an t-olc,
marbh didhiu mé féin,
ná marbh mo mhac!
Mo chíocha gan loim,
mo shúile go fliuch,
mo lámha ar crith,
mo chorpán gan níth,
mo chéile gan mhac,
mé féine gan neart,
mo bheatha is fiú bás!
Uch, m'aonmhac, a Dhé!
M'fhaoidhe gan luach,
mo ghalar gan ghein,
gan díoghail go bráth;
mo chíocha 'na dtost,
mo chridhe ro chrom.

Ben Aile: Aon shiorthaoi dá mharbhadh,
sochaidhe mharbhthaoi,
naoidhin bhuailtí,
na haithreacha ghontaoi,
na máithreacha mharbhthaoi,
ifreann ro líon sibh
neamh ro dhún sibh,
fola fírén
ro dhoirtseabhar gan chionaidh.

Ben Aile: Tair chugam, a Chríost,
beir m'anmain go luath
maraon is mo mhac!
Uch, a Mhuire mhór,

He drank of my breast,
My womb that carried him,
He sucked of my vitals,
He soothed my heart,
My life – it was he,
My death to take him from me.
It has drained all my strength,
It has stilled my speech,
It has darkened my eyes.

Another Woman: It's my son you take from me;
'Tisn't he has done wrong.
Then kill me myself,
But do not kill my son!
My breasts without milk,
My eyes wet with tears,
My hands all a-tremble,
My body without pith,
My husband without a son,
Myself without strength,
My life is but death.
Alas, O God, my one son!
My cries are in vain.
My grief, and I childless,
Till Doom unavenged.
My breasts are stilled,
My heart is bowed down.

Another Woman: You seek one to kill;
– You kill many:
Babes you strike down,
The fathers you wound,
The mothers you slay,
Hell you have filled,
Heaven you've closed,
Blood you have spilled
Of the just without guilt.

Another Woman: Come to me, Christ!
Take quickly my life
Along with my son!
O great Mary,

83

Máthair Mheic Dé,
ciodh do-dhéan gan mhac?
Tríd Mhacsa ro marbhadh
mo chonn is mo chiall;
do-rinne bean bhaoth díom
i ndiaidh mo mheic;
mo chridhe is caob cró
a haithle an áir thruaigh
ó 'ndiu go dtí bráth.

17. A Bhean Lán de Stuaim

A bhean lán de stuaim
    coingibh uaim do lámh;
ní fear gníomha sinn
    cé taoi tinn dar ngrádh.

Féach ar liath dem fholt,
    féach mo chorp gan lúth,
féach ar thraoch dem fhuil –
    créad re bhfuil do thnúth?

Ná saoil mé go saobh,
    arís ná claon do cheann;
bíodh ar ngrádh gan ghníomh
    go bráth, a shíodh sheang.

Druid do bhéal óm bhéal –
    doiligh an scéal do chor –
ná bíom cneas re cneas:
    tig ón teas an tol.

Do chúl craobhach cas,
    do rosc glas mar dhrúcht,
do chíoch chruinngheal bhláith
    tharraingeas mian súl.

Mother of the Son of God,
What shall I do without a son?
On account of your Son
My reason and sense have been killed;
I have become crazed
In the wake of my son.
My heart's a clot of blood
After the piteous slaughter
From this day till Doom.

17. O Woman Full of Grace

Our seventeenth-century Bardic poem by Keating looks formally complete
without the two additional stanzas in song metre which I omit here:

O woman full of grace,
    Keep your hand from me;
I am not one for deeds,
    Though for my love you crave.

See my hair all grey,
    My body without motion,
My blood exhausted, pale,
    For what are you hoping?

Think not I'm perverse,
    Your head no more incline,
Let our love unacted be
    For ever, slender sprite!

Take your lips from mine!
    Hard, hard to tell it right –
Let not your skin commune with mine,
    From heat flows desire.

Your branching, curling hair,
    Your grey eye like dew,
Your bright rounded smooth breast
    Fire men's eyes for you.

Gach gníomh acht gníomh cuirp
is luighe id chuilt shuain
do-ghéan féin tréd ghrádh,
a bhean lán de stuaim.

18. Ní Bhfuighe Mise Bás Duit

Ní bhfuighe mise bás duit,
    a bhean úd an chuirp mar ghéis;
daoine leamha ar mharbhais riamh,
    ní hionann iad is mé féin.

Créad umá rachainn-se d'éag
    don bhéal dearg, don déad mar bhláth?
an crobh míolla, an t-ucht mar aol,
    an dáibh do-gheabhainn féin bás?

Do mhéin aobhdha, th'aigneadh saor,
    a bhas thana, a thaobh mar chuip,
a rosg gorm, a brágha bhán –
    ní bhfuighe mise bás duit.

Do chíocha corra, a chneas úr,
    do ghruaidh chorcra, do chúl fiar, –
go deimhin ní bhfuighead bás
    dóibh sin go madh háil le Dia.

Do mhala chaol, t'fholt mar ór,
    do rún geanmnaidh, do ghlór leasg,
do shál chruinn, do cholpa réidh, –
    ní mhuirbhfeadh siad acht duine leamh.

A bhean úd an chuirp mar ghéis,
    do hoileadh mé ag duine glic;
aithne dham mar bhíd na mná;
    ní bhfuighe mise bás duit!

Every act but that of love,
   Lying in your slumbrous counterpane,
I would do for your love,
   O woman full of grace.

18. I Shall Not Die for Thee

The renunciation of love in such a vein as appears in this Irish poem was a rather common theme with sixteenth-century English poets like Wyatt and Surrey. Bilingual poets such as William Nugent/ Liam Nuinseann of Delvin, Westmeath, would have made the overlap easily possible.

I shall not die for thee,
   O woman shaped like the swan,
'Tis foolish men you've ever killed,
   – They are not the same as me.

Why should I taste death
   For red lips, for flower-bright teeth?
For graceful hand and lime-white breast
   – Is it for these I should die?

Your gracious bent, your noble mind,
   O slender hand, O foam-like form,
White neck and deep-blue eye,
   I shall not die for thee.

Your tapering breasts, O bright-skinned one,
   Your curling hair, your purple cheek,
I surely shall not die,
   Until God wills, for these.

Your slender brow, your hair like gold,
   Your modest heart, voice languid, cool,
Rounded heel and smooth-arched calf
   Would kill none but a fool.

O woman shaped like the swan,
   A wise one fostered me,
I know how women are;
   I shall not die for thee!

19. 'Sí Mo Ghrádh

'Sí mo ghrádh
an bhean is mó bhíos dom chrádh;
annsa í óm dhéanamh tinn
ná an bhean do-ghéanadh sinn slán.

'Sí mo shearc
bean nár fhágaibh ionnam neart,
bean nách léigfeadh im dhiaidh och,
bean nách cuirfeadh cloch im leacht.

'Sí mo stór
bean an ruisg uaine mar phór,
bean nách cuirfeadh lámh fám chionn,
bean nách luighfeadh liom ar ór.

'Sí mo rún
bean nách innseann éinní dhún,
bean nách cloiseann ní fán ngréin,
bean nách déin orm silleadh súl.

Mór mo chás,
iongna a fhad go bhfaghaim bás;
an bhean nách tiubhradh taobh liom,
dar mo mhionn, isí mo ghrádh.

20. Léig Díot t'Airm

19. My Love

In this poem the early modern Bardic poet resolves his love paradox in five stanzas, without, apparently, taking it too much to heart.

My love is she
– The woman that most vexes me,
  Dearer she my health would ruin
Than the one would work my cure.

My darling she
– The one that took my strength away,
  One that would not sigh for me,
Or place a stone upon my grave.

My sweetheart she
– The one of the bean-green eye,
  Who would never encircle my head with her arm,
Nor sleep at all by my side.

My dearest she
Who never tells a thing to me,
  Who never hears a mortal thing,
Who never casts an eye on me.

Sad my plight!
Wondrous long 'tis till I die!
  The one that would not lie with me
Is the one, I vow, for whom I sigh.

20. Lay Down Your Arms
(Piaras Feiritéar, †1653)

Of an old Norman-Irish family seated in the extreme west of the Dingle peninsula, Piaras Feiritéar (Pierce Ferriter), a prototype of west Kerry versatility, was poet, musician, soldier and leader of his people in his time. He took a prominent part in the west Kerry campaign on the Irish side against the English during the war of 1641-1653. In the latter year he was treacherously taken while negotiating under safe conduct with the English and hanged in Killarney.

Léig díot t'airm, a mhacaoimh mná,
  muna fearr leat cách do lot;
muna léigir th'airm-se dhíot,
  cuirfead bannaí dáirithe ort.

Má chuireann tú th'airm ar gcúl,
  foiligh feasta do chúl cas,
ná léig leis do bhrághaid bhán
  nár léig duine do chách as.

Má shíleann tú féin, a bhean,
  nár mharbhais aon theas ná thuaidh,
do mharbh silleadh do shúl rín
  cách uile gan sgín gan tuaigh.

Dar leat acht cé maol do ghlún,
  dar fós acht cé húr do ghlac,
do loitsead a bhfacaidh iad –
  ní fearra dhuit sgiath is ga.

Foiligh oram th'ucht mar aol,
  ná feicear fós do thaobh nocht;
ar ghrádh Chríost ná feiceadh cách
  do chíogh rógheal mar bhláth dos.

Foiligh oram do rosg rín,
  má théid ar mharbhais dínn leat;
ar ghrádh th'anma dún do bhéal,
  ná feiceadh aon do dhéad gheal.

Más leór leat ar chuiris tim,
  sul a gcuirthear sinn i gcré,
a bhean atá rem ro-chlaoi,
  na hairm-sin díotsa léig.

Lay down your arms, young lady,
  Unless you'd rather slay us all!
If you do not lay your arms down,
  I will bind you on terms of bail.

If you put your arms there behind,
  Then henceforth hide your curling hair;
Leave not your white throat bare
  That has never let anyone escape.

Lady, if you yourself conceive
  That south or north not one you've slain,
– The glance of your stately eye has slain
  Every last one without axe or knife.

Although you may think your knee is bare
  And the palm of your hand no way hard,
They've vanquished all that saw them,
  – What better were shield and spear?

Your lime-white bosom from me hide,
  Let your body not be seen bare,
For Christ's love let no one see
  Your breast snow-white like blossom on tree.

Your stately eye from me hide,
  If all of us you've killed are with you now,
For your soul's love close your lips,
  Let no one see your white teeth.

If you think it enough you've enfeebled,
  – Before we are put into the ground,
O lady would utterly vanquish me,
  Lay those arms down!

Modern Irish Triads and Proverbs

21. Tréanna

1. Na trí riain is giorra fhanas: rian éin ar chraoibh, rian bric ar linn, rian fir ar mhnaoi.

2. Na trí nithe bhíos geal ina dtosach, breac ina lár agus dubh ina ndeireadh: comhar, cleamhnas, éintíos.

3. Na trí beaga is fearr: beag na curcóige, beag na caorach is beag na mná.

4. Na trí nithe is fuaire ar bith: glúin fir, srón con, cíoch mhná.

5. Trí éirghe is measa do-ghní duine: éirghe ó aifreann gan chríochnú, éirghe ó bhia gan altú, agus éirghe óna mhnaoi féin go nuig a hatharú.

6. Na trí rudaí nar fhéad Aristatl dul amach orthu: líonadh agus trá na taoide, obair na mbeach, agus intinn mná.

7. Trí ní nach féidir a fheiscint: faobhar, gaoth, agus grá.

8. Na trí nithe is measa i dtigh: báirseach mná, simné deataigh agus sú sileáin.

9. Trí nithe ná fuil seansúil: bean bhreá, bó bhán, nó tigh ar ard.

10. Trí ní nár chóir amharc air: cailín Domhnaigh, bó shamhraidh, agus caora fhómhair.

11. Trí nithe chomh maith le nithe is fearr ná iad: claíomh adhmaid ag fear meata, bean ghránna ag dall, drochéadach ar dhrúncaer.

12. Na trí nithe is gránna ina gcineál féin: bean chaol rua, capall caol buí, bó chaol bhán.

13. Na trí ní is súgaí amuigh: pisín cait, mionnán gabhair, baintreach óg mná.

14. Na trí nithe is ríméadaí: garra fataí fána bhláth bán, long fá sheol, bean thar éis oidhre óig.

15. Triúr is géire radharc: seabhac ar chrann, cú i ngleann, nó cailín i lár cruinnithe.

16. Na trí rudaí is géire amuigh: fiacail con, focal amadáin, nó súil mná óige i ndiaidh óigfhir.

21. Modern Irish Triads

1. The three most short-lived traces: the trace of a bird on a branch, the trace of a fish on a pool, and the trace of a man on a woman.
2. The three things that are bright in the beginning, speckled in the middle and black in the end: co-operation in farm-work, a marriage alliance, living together.
3. The three best small things: a small beehive, a small sheep, a small woman.
4. The three coldest things: a man's knee, a hound's nose, a woman's breast.
5. The three worst risings: rising from Mass before it is finished, rising from food without saying grace, and rising from one's own wife for another woman.
6. The three things Aristotle could not understand: the flow and ebb of the tide, the labour of the bees, and the mind of woman.
7. Three things that cannot be seen: the edge of a blade, the wind, love.
8. The three worst things in a house: a scolding wife, a smoking chimney, and falling soot.
9. Three things that are not lucky: a handsome woman, a white cow, a house on a height.
   (They may fall victim to the Evil Eye, through envy.)
10. Three things that should not be looked upon: a girl on Sunday, a cow in Summer, and a sheep in Autumn.
    (When they look their best they are most vulnerable to the Evil Eye.)
11. Three things that are as good as better things: a wooden sword in the hands of a coward, an ugly wife to a blind man, poor clothes on a drunkard.
12. The three ugliest things of their kind: a thin red-haired woman, a thin yellow horse, a thin white cow.
13. The three most light-hearted things in the world: a kitten, a kid, a young widow.
14. The three gladdest things: a potato-field in white flower, a ship in full sail, a woman who has given birth to a son.
15. The three with the sharpest vision: a hawk on a tree, a hound in a valley, or a girl in the middle of a gathering.
16. The three sharpest things in the world: the tooth of a hound, the word of a fool, or the eye of a young woman after a young man.

17. Cuid na mná: an chuid is crua den leaba, an chuid is caoile den mbeatha, an chuid is reímhre den mbata.

18. Na trí rud is deacra a phiocadh: bean, speal is rásúr.

19. Trí shórt ban nach féidir le fear a dtuiscint: bean óg, bean mheánaosta, seanbhean.

22. Seanfhocail na Muimhneach

1. Ar mo ghabháil amach ar maidin
   Do bhuail an bhean rua liom,
   Chonac an giorria dubh ar an drúcht,
   Chuala an chuach im' chúl,
   Agus annsan d'aithiníos
   Ná beadh an bhliain sin liúm.

2. Díogha gach tine an fhearnóg úr,
   Díogha gach síne an flichshneachta fuar,
   Díogha gach dí an mheadhg shean,
   Agus díogha gach díogha drochbhean.

3. Deireadh fir a shuan, is an bhean á faire féin.
   For another version see SM No. 14.

4. Coileach bán ar chearcaibh,
   Nó file mná i mbaile.

5. Is fearrde bean leanbh, is ní miste di beirt.
   For another version see SM No. 59.

6. Tabhair do ghrá dod' mhnaoi
   Is do rún dod' mháthair.

17. Woman's lot: the hardest part of the bed, the slightest share
    of the food, the thickest part of the stick.
    (This rhetorical version by a woman is not meant too seriously.)
18. The three things that are hardest to pick: a woman, a scythe,
    a razor.
19. Three kinds of woman that a man cannot understand: a young
    woman, a middle-aged woman, an old woman.

22. Munster Proverbs

1. In the morning on my way
   I met the red-haired woman;
   I saw the black hare upon the dew,
   I heard the cuckoo behind me,
   And then I knew
   That year I would be in for a bad time.

Superstitions such as these, called freets *in the north,* pishogues *in the west
and* pistrogues *elsewhere in Ireland, used to be quite common.*

2. The worst of fires is fresh alder wood,
   The worst of weathers is cold sleet,
   The worst of drinks is old whey,
   And the worst of all is a bad woman.

3. For a man the end is sleep, while the woman wakes and
   watches.

*The reference here is either to the end of life, or to the end of sexual intercourse.
Men appear to favour the latter interpretation.*

4. A white cock among hens
   Or a woman poet in a village.

These are taken to be undesirable.

5. A woman is the better of having one child and is none the
   worse of a second.

The argument, then, is for two at most.

6. Love your wife
   And confide in your mother.

97

7. Ná bac éinne ná bíonn buíochas na mban air.

8. Cion i gan fhios do mhnaoi nó leanbh.

9. Iarr ar mhnaoi é uair nó dhó,
   Is mara dtagaid leat tar leo.

10. Níl aon leaghadh Dia ná faigheann lom-angar.

11. Céad ghrá mná, dara grá fir.
    See also SM No. 234.

12. Bás na céad mhná nó báisteach tar éis dinnéir.

13. Ma táim-se geanncach, teannfar púint liom.

14. Imíonn an spré leis a' bhfaill,
    Ach fanann an bhreill ar an mnaoi.

15. Is mac do mhac go bpósair é,
    Ach is iníon t'iníon go dtéir sa chré.

16. Adú tine le loch,
    Caitheamh cloch in aghaidh cuain,
    Comhairle 'thabhairt do mhnaoi bhuirb,
    Nó buille ribe ar iarann fhuar.

7. Take little account of anyone that the womenfolk do not respect.

8. Love of woman or child should be kept secret.
It is felt that otherwise the one who loves may be exploited.

9. Ask a woman once or twice
And if they will not come, go with them.

The Mating of Hard Cases

10. There's no ne'er-do-well but finds a corresponding mate.
Leaghadh Dia lit. God's melting: a ne'er-do-well; lom-angar lit. naked necessity: a destitute person.

The Rating of Spouses

11. A woman's first love, a man's second.
These are what count most.

12. The first wife's death, or rain after dinner.
These are but minor calamities!

Money and Beauty

13. If I am snub-nosed, I'll be given a greater dowry.

14. Her fortune falls down the cliff,
But the bride's wry mouth remains.

A Daughter's Constancy

15. Your son is your son till he marries a wife,
But your daughter's your daughter all your life.

Fruitless Tasks

16. Kindling fire by a lake,
Flinging stones into the bay,
Counselling a woman that's crude,
Or striking cold iron with a single grass blade.

17. Cailín ag Móir, is Mór ag iarraidh déirce.

18. Iníon na bunóirsí
    Abhar na hóinsí.

19. Síodaí buí ar Shiobhán,
    Is na preabáin ar a hathair.

23. Seanfhocla Chonnacht

1. Má phósann tú bean fhionn, tá na súile ró-chlaon aici,
   Má phósann tú bean bhuí, beidh síolrach gan scéimh aici,
   Má phósann tú bean rua, is gearrr é do shaol aici,
   Ach i bpáirt na mná duibhe í, 'sí fuíollach fear Éireann í.

2. Dá mba lachain san uisce na cailíní deasa,
   Bheadh sciatháin ar bhuachaillí ag eiteall 'na n-aice,
   Dá mba loin dubha móra iad nó smólaigh buí breaca,
   Bheadh buachaillí óga á dtóraíocht 'sna sceacha.

3. Comhfhad fuacht 's teas,
   Comhfhad fuath 's grá,
   Ach téann an t-éad go dtí an smior,
   'S fanann ann go brách.

4. Ní fhaca mé bean riamh a' teacht chuig an tine
   Nach gcorródh sí í is nach gcuirfeadh sí a cuma féin uirthi.

5. Tógann sé fiche bliain de mhnaoi fear a dhéanamh dá mac,
   Ach ní thógann sé ach fiche móiméad de mhnaoi eile amadán
   a dhéanamh de.

100

Contrasts

17. Mór, though a beggar, has a maid.
Mór, originally a goddess, is here the type of the peasant woman.

18. The industrious woman's daughter
    Is the makings of a thriftless girl.

19. In yellow silks Shivawn is clad
    And nought but rags upon her dad.

23. Connacht Proverbs

1. *The Fastidious Bachelor*
If you marry a fair-haired woman, her eyes are too crooked,
If the one you marry is yellow-haired, her children won't be much
    to look at,
If you marry a red-haired one, she'll soon be the death of you,
And as for the dark-haired one, she's everybody's reject.

2. *Attraction*
If the pretty girls were ducks swimming,
The boys would grow wings and fly with them,
If they were large blackbirds or speckled yellow thrushes,
The young lads would be pursuing them into the bushes.

3. *Jealousy*
Heat extends as far as cold
And love as far as hate,
But jealousy to the marrow goes
And stays forever there.

4. *Signature*
I never saw a woman come nigh to the fire
But she stirred it and shaped it to her heart's desire.

5. *Timescales*
One woman takes twenty years to make a man of her son
And another but twenty minutes to make a fool of him.

6. Ní ólann na mná fíon
   Ach imíonn sé lena linn.

7. Tús grá síordhearcadh.

8. Rinne sí a grá ach ní dhearna sí a goradh.

9a. A bhuachaill, beidh tú buartha go bpósair,
    'S uaidh sin ní suaimhneas go deo dhuit,
    Mar ní féasta go rósta,
    Is ní céasta go pósta.

9b. Ón lá a phósas duine,
    Bíonn a chroí ina bhéal
    'S a lámh ina phóca.

10. Is dubhach don teach
    Nuair ghlaos an chearc
    Níos aoirde ná'n coileach.

11. Ná codail aon oíche go deo
    I dteach a mbeidh bean óg
    Pósta ag seanduine.

12. Pós bean aniar
    Agus pósfair a bhfuil thiar.

13. Ná cuir fear óg ag iarraidh mná dhuit féin.

14a. Ná pós bean ar a spré,
     'S ná pós bean gan é.

6. *Mystery*
Women do not drink wine,
But it vanishes in their time.

7. *Love's Beginning*
Constant watching is the beginning of love.

8. *Unprofitable Marriage*
She won her love but not her fortune.
Literally: She made [attained] her love but not her warming.

9a. My lad, you'll be sad till you're wed,
And thereafter you'll ne'er rest your head,
For without a roast there's no banquet,
And no anguish until marriage.

9b. From the day a person weds
His heart is in his mouth
And his hand is in his poke.

10. *The Dominant Wife*
'Tis sad for the house
When the hen crows
Louder than the cock.

11. *Old Men are Jealous*
Never sleep any night in a house
Where an old man
Has a young spouse.

12. *The Close-Knit Community*
Marry a woman from the West
And you'll marry all the rest.

13. *Your Matchmaker As Rival*
Don't send a young man to ask the woman for you.

14a. *Her Fortune*
Don't marry a woman for her fortune,
And don't marry one without it.

14b. Tá a spré i gclár a héadain.

15. Níl cleamhnas ar bith is fearr rath
    Ná cleamhnas na luaithe.

16. Ní bhíonn sé ina cheol i gcónaí ag bean an phíobaire.

24. Seanfhocla Uladh

1. Is amhlaidh bhíos an bhean:
   Gibé fear ann a gcuireann spéis,
   Ní hannsa léi an séimh saor
   Nó an duine daor dubh dá éis.

2. Is í an óige an bhean mhaiseach,
   Is í an aois a' dúchosach,
   Is í an tsláinte an rua-fhrasach,
   Is é an saol an fear cleasach.

3. Sláinte 'gus saol agat,
   Bean ar do mhian agat,
   Talamh gan cíos agat,
   Leanbh gach bliain agat,
   Airgead síos agat,
   Ón mhí seo amach!

4. Bíonn na mrá ag obair is na fir ag amhanc uaofa.

5. Ná bí a choíche i gcúirt nó i gcaisleán
   Gan mnaoi a thabhairt do leithscéil.

14b. Her fortune is in her forehead.
A beautiful woman needs no fortune.

15. *Marry A Neighbour*
No match at all is luckier
Than the ashpit match.

16. *No Bed Of Roses*
It's not all music for the piper's wife.

24. Ulster Proverbs

1. *First Love*
This is how a woman is:
Whatever man she comes to like,
No dearer to her afterwards
Is dark serf or gentle knight.

2. *Profiles*
Youth is a woman in all her beauty,
Age has feet that are black,
Health is an almighty spender,
The world is a man full of tricks and knacks.

3. *A Toast*
Health and long life to you!
A woman you'd like to you!
Land without rent to you!
A baby each year to you!
Cash in your hand
From this very month!

4. *Life on Tory Island as Seen by a Woman*
The women work and the men look into the distance.

5. *Advice to a Young Man*
In court or in castle never be found
Without a woman to speak on your account.

6. An bhean bhán: mar bheadh an lán amach is isteach,
   An bhean dubh: mar d'imeodh an t-uisce ón trá,
   An bhean donn: mar bheadh long ar uisce ghlan.

7. Folaíonn grá gráin,
   Is tchí fuath a lán.

8. Losg sí a gual is cha dtearn sí a goradh.

9. Féach an ceann 's gan ann ach áit na súl,
   Féach an dranndal manntach bearnach gan lúth,
   's a spéirbhean deas na mbánchíoch álainn úr,
   Beidh do cheann-sa feannta ar lár mar siúd.

10. Praiseach buí na ngort
    Chuireas mná na Mí le holc.

11. Is furas brídeog dhóighiúil a chóiriú.

12. Chan fhuil rún anois ann, ó tá sé ag mnaoi.

6. *Sea Imagery*
The flaxen-haired woman: like the tide at the full out and in;
The dark-haired woman: like the water ebbing from the shore;
The brown-haired woman: like a ship on clear water.

7. *Love and Hate*
Concealed beneath love lies hate
And hate sees much (to blame).

8. *A Bad Marriage*
She has burnt her coal without heating herself.

9. *Memento Mori*
See the skull with gaping chasms for the eyes,
See the gapped mouth motionless and wide,
O lovely lady of the chalk-white shapely breasts,
Your head so flayed one day in dust must rest.

10. *Love and Brassica*
The brassica of the fields
Is what brings the women of Meath to grief.
Gathering this herb was said to be the pretext for meeting lovers.

11. *Beauty Needs no Aids*
A comely bride is easily dressed.

12. *Can You Keep a Secret?*
It's no longer a secret – it's been told to a woman.

Modern Irish Songs and Poems

25. A Ógánaigh an Chúil Cheangailte

A ógánaigh an chúil cheangailte
  le raibh mé seal in éineacht,
chuaidh tú aréir an bealach seo
  is ní tháinic tú dom fhéachaint.
Shíl mé nach ndéanfaí dochar duit
  dá dtagthá agus mé d'iarraidh,
is gurb í do phóigín a thabharfadh sólás dom
  dá mbeinn i lár an fhiabhrais.

Dá mbeadh maoin agamsa
  agus airgead 'mo phóca,
dhéanfainn bóithrín aicearrach
  go doras tí mo stóirín,
mar shúil le Dia go gcluinfinnse
  torann binn a bhróige,
's is fada ón lá 'nar chodail mé
  ach ag súil le blas a phóige.

Agus shíl mé, a stóirín,
  go mba gealach agus grian thú,
agus shíl mé ina dhiaidh sin
  go mba sneachta ar an tsliabh thú,
agus shíl mé ina dhiaidh sin
  go mba lóchrann ó Dhia thú,
nó go mba tú an réalt eólais
  ag dul romham is 'mo dhiaidh thú.

Gheall tú síoda is saitin dom,
  callaí agus bróga arda,
is gheall tú tar a éis sin
  go leanfá tríd an tsnámh mé.
Ní mar sin atá mé
  ach 'mo sceach i mbéal bearna
gach nóin agus gach maidin
  ag féachaint tí mo mháthar.

25. O Youth of the Loose-Bound Hair

In this effective and moving song familiar folk imagery is used to convey the girl's idealisation of her beloved and her sorrow at being abandoned by him.

O youth of the loose-bound hair,
    With whom I once kept company,
Last night you came this way
    But did not visit me;
I thought it would not harm you
    To come and ask for me,
For your kiss would give me solace
    If I were in a burning fever.

If I had property
    And money to my hand,
I'd make a short-cut boreen
    To the doorway of my dear,
Hoping I might hear
    The sweet sound of his footfall,
For long I have not slept at all
    Hoping to taste his kiss.

I had thought, O my dear,
    That you were sun and moon,
And thought after that
    That you were snow on the moor,
And thought after that
    You were God's own guiding light,
Or the star of knowledge
    Going before me and behind.

You promised silk and satin,
    Fine clothes and high-heeled shoes,
And after that you promised
    To follow me through rough and smooth.
Instead I am left all alone,
    Like a bush in the mouth of a gap,
Tending my mother's home
    Each morning and each evening.

26. Dónall Óg

A Dhónaill Óig, má théir thar farraige,
Beir mé féin leat, as ná déan mo dhearmad;
As beidh agat féirín lá aonaigh is margaidh,
Is iníon rí Gréige mar chéile leapa agat.

Má théir-se anonn, tá comhartha agam ort:
Tá cúl fionn agus dhá shúil ghlasa agat,
Dhá chocán déag i do chúl buí bachallach,
Mar bheadh béal na bó nó rós i ngarraithe.

Is déanach aréir do labhair an gadhar ort,
Do labhair an naoscach sa churraichín doimhin ort,
Is tú id chaonaí aonair ar fud na gcoillte,
Is go rabhair gan chéile go héag go bhfaghair me!

Do gheallais domh-sa, agus d'innsis bréag dom,
Go mbeitheá romham-sa ag cró na gcaorach;
Do leigeas fead agus trí chéad ghlaoch chút,
Is ní bhfuaras ann ach uan ag méiligh.

Do gheallais domh-sa ní ba dheacair duit:
Loingeas óir fá chrann seoil airgid,
Dhá bhaile dhéag de bhailtibh margaidh,
Is cúirt bhreágh aolga cois taobh na farraige.

Do gheallais domh-sa ní nár bhféidir,
Go dtabharfá lámhainne de chroiceann éisc dom,
Go dtabharfá bróga de chroiceann éan dom,
Is culaith den tsíoda ba dhaoire in Éirinn.

A Dhónaill Óig, b'fhearr duit mise agat
Ná bean uasal uaibhreach iomarcach;
Do chrúfainn bó is do dhéanfainn cuigeann duit,
Is dá mba chruaidh é bhuailfinn buille leat.

26. Donal Óg

*This celebrated song is a classic example of the Irish folksong and is found in
different versions throughout the area of Gaelic tradition from Munster to
Scotland. Employing with great effect the varied imagery of the Irish
countryside and seaside, it convinces by its note of sincerity, particularly in
stanza 11 and in the impressive final stanza.*

O Donal Óg, if you go oversea,
Take myself with you – and do not forget me!
And you'll have a keepsake on fair and market day,
And the Greek king's daughter as your bedmate.

If you go over, I have your mark:
You have a head of fair hair and two grey eyes,
Twelve curls in your yellow ringlets behind,
The cowslip or the garden rose – that would be their like.

The dog cried out to you late last night,
From the depths of the quagmire cried the snipe,
You were moving all alone through the woodlands wild,
And I pray that you will never wed until you are mine.

You promised me – 'twas the lie you told –
That you'd be before me at the sheepfold,
I whistled and called out to you three hundred times,
But the bleating of the lone lamb was all I got in reply.

You promised me a thing right hard:
A ship of gold with a silver mast,
Twelve towns where markets are wont to be,
And a fair limed court beside the sea.

You promised what could never be,
That you'd give me gloves of the skin of fish,
That you'd give me boots of the skin of birds,
And a suit of the dearest Irish silk.

O Donal Óg, you'd be better with me
Than with a noblewoman, proud and haughty,
I'd milk the cow for you and do the churning,
And strike a blow with you if your need was urgent.

Och, ochón! agus ní le hocras,
Uireasa bí, dí ná codlata
Fá ndear domh-sa bheith tanaí triuchalga,
Ach grá fir óig is é bhreoigh go follas mé.

Is moch ar maidin do chonnac-sa an t-óigfhear
Ar muin chapaill ag gabháil an bhóthair,
Níor dhruid sé liom is níor chuir ná streo orm,
Is ar mo chasadh abhaile dhom sea ghoileas mo dhóthain.

Nuair théim-se féin go Tobar an Uaignis
Suím síos ag déanamh buartha,
Nuair chím an saol is ná feicim mo bhuachaill,
Go raibh scáil an ómair i mbarr a ghruanna.

Siúd é an Domhnach do thugas grá duit,
An Domhnach díreach roimh Domhnach Cásca,
Is mise ar mo ghlúinibh ag léamh na Páise,
Sea bhí mo dhá shúil ag síor-thabhairt an ghrá dhuit.

Dúirt mo mháithrín liom gan labhairt leat
Inniu ná amárach ná Dia Domhnaigh.
Is olc an tráth do thug sí rabhadh dom
's é dúnadh an dorais é i ndiaidh na foghla.

Ó a dhe, a mháithrín, tabhair mé féin dó.
Is tabhair a bhfuil agat den tsaol go léir dó;
Éirigh féin ag iarraidh déirce,
Agus ná gabh siar ná aniar ar m'éileamh.

Do bhainis soir dhíom, is do bhainis siar dhíom,
Do bhainis romham is do bhainis im'dhiaidh dhíom,
Do bhainis gealach is do bhainis grian díom,
's is ró-mhór m'eagla gur bhainis Dia dhíom.

Woe, alas! Not from hunger,
Lack of food or drink or sleep
That I am pining, pinched and peaked,
But a young man's love has wasted me.

In the early morning I saw the young man
Riding on horseback along the road;
He didn't come near me and he gave no greeting,
And I cried my fill as I turned back home.

Whenever I go to the Well of Loneliness,
I sit me down and take to mourning,
When I see all the world except only my dear,
With the shade of amber high on his cheeks.

That was the Sunday I gave my love to your keeping,
At the Mass of the Palms before Sunday of Easter,
Christ's Passion of branches on my knees I was reading,
But my two eyes were on you and my heart was bleeding.

My mother has told me not to speak to you,
Today nor tomorrow nor on Sunday:
'Twas an ill time she gave me her caution –
Closing the door after the robbing.

O darling mother, give me away to him,
And give all you have in the whole wide world to him,
Go out yourself with the beggar's bowl,
And grant what I ask without toing and froing.

You've taken east from me, you've taken west from me,
The road behind me, and the road before,
You've taken moon, you've taken sun from me,
And I'm in dread you've taken the God I adore.

27. Caiseal Mumhan

Phósfainn thú gan bha gan phúnt gan áireamh spré,
agus phógfainn thú maidin drúchta le bánú an lae.
'S é mo ghalar dúch gan mé is tú, a dhianghrá mo chléibh,
i gCaiseal Mumhan is gan de leaba fúinn ach clár bog déil.

Siúil, a chogair, is tar a chodladh liom féin sa ghleann;
gheóbhaidh tú foscadh, leaba fhlocais is aer cois abhann;
beidh na srotha ag gabháil thorainn faoi ghéaga crann;
beidh an londubh inár bhfochair is an chéirseach dhonn.

Searc mo chléibh a thug mé féin duit is grá trí rún,
's go dtaga sé de chor sa tsaol dom bheith lá 'gus tú
is ceangal cléire eadrainn araon is an fáinne dlúth;
's dá bhfeicfinn féin mo shearc ag aon fhear gheóbhainn bás le
cumha.

28. A Bhuachaill an Chúil Dualaigh

A bhuachaill an chúil dualaigh,
    Cár chodail mé 'réir?
Ag colú do leapan,
    'S níor airigh tú mé.
Dá mbeadh fios mo cháis agat,

27. Cashel of Munster *or* The Soft Deal Board

In rural Ireland elopement or the runaway match developed as a counterpoise to the institution of made matches. To persuade their parents that they had better be allowed marry, it was sufficient for the lovers to absent themselves together overnight. The bride traditionally supplied the bedclothes, including the mattress. In this popular song with the double title, the lover and prospective husband will be glad to forego the bride's contribution: the bed will then be of softwood of the cheapest kind, namely deal *(pronounced* dale *in most dialects). The suggestion that* bog deal *is involved here and consequently in the title, appears to lack foundation.*

I'd wed you, dear, without cows or gear, or pounds to pay,
And I'd kiss you on a dewy morn at day-dawn grey.
My grief tonight! – Were but you and I, O dearest one, away
In Cashel of Munster with no bed under us but a soft board of
    dale.

Come, my dear, and sleep with me down in the glen,
Where you'll find shelter, a downy bed and an airy stream,
The waters gliding by us under branching trees,
The blackbird and his brown consort in our company.

All my love I gave to you, from the world concealed,
– And may it chance one day that you and I allied will be,
The cleric's tie upon our lives with the ring to seal,
– And if I saw my dear to another wed, O, I would die of grief.

28. O Youth of the Ringlets

This song has been recorded in Munster and, with slight modification of text, in Galway. The love theme is firmly and competently handled and the plight of the love-lorn girl convincingly presented.

    O youth of the ringlets
        Where did I sleep last night?
    – You did not hear me,
        Though I slept by your own bedside.
    If you knew my sad story

Ní chodlófá néal,
'S gurab é do chómhrá binn blasta
D'fhág an osna so im thaobh.

Nuair luím ar mo leabain
'Sí m'aisling ochón,
'S ar m'éirghe dham ar maidin
'Sí mo phaidir mo dheór.
Mo ghruaig bhí 'n-a dualaibh
Is d'imigh 'n-a ceó,
'Chionn grá 'thúirt don bhuachaill
Nach bhfuighead-sa go deó!

A bhuachaill an chúil dualaigh,
    Nár fheice mé Dia
Go bhfeicim-se do sgáile
    'Teacht 'dir mé is an ghrian!
Ní thuigeann tú mo mhearú,
    'S ní airíonn tú mo phian,
Is mar bharr ar gach aindeis
    Is leat do chailleas mo chiall!

A bhuachaill an chúil dualaigh,
    An bhfuil ár sonas le fáil,
Nó a' mbeimid 'n-ár gcomhnuí
    In aon lóisdín amháin?
Sinn araon pósda,
    A stóir 's a dhian-ghrá,
Ár náimhdibh fá bhrón,
    Is ár gcómhgas go sámh!

29. An Cuimhin Leat an Oíche Úd?

An cuimhin leat an oíche úd
    Do bhí tú ag an bhfuinneóg,
Gan hata, gan laimhnne
    Dhod dhíon, gan chasóg?

118

You would not get a wink of sleep,
'Tis your sweet and fluent conversation
That makes my heart grieve.

When I lie on my pallet,
My dreaming is to sigh,
My praying is weeping
In the morning when I rise.
My hair that was in ringlets
Has melted like the mist,
All from loving the dear lad
That never will be mine.

O youth of the ringlets
May I never see God
Until I see your shadow
Come between me and the sun!
You do not know my frenzy,
You do not feel my pain,
And to crown all my afflictions,
You have maddened my brain.

O youth of the ringlets,
Is our happiness to be found?
Or will we ever live
Together in one house?
In wedlock united,
O darling I love best,
Our enemies slighted
And our friends at rest!

29. You Remember that Night?

This Munster song gives an eloquent account of a girl's love for a young man and of her hopes for their future together.

You remember that night, dear,
You were at the window,
Without hat, without gloves,
Nor coat on to shield you?

Do shín mé mo lámh chút,
  'S do rug tú uirthi barróg,
Is d'fhan mé id chomhluadar
  Nó gur labhair an fhuiseóg!

An cuimhin leat an oíche úd
  Do bhí tú agus mise
Ag bun an chrainn chaorthainn
  'S an oíche a' cur chuisne?
Do cheann ar mo chíochaibh,
  Is do phíob gheal dhá seinm,
Is beag do shaoileas an oíche úd
  Go sgaoilfeadh ár gcumann!

A chumainn mo chroí 'stigh,
  Tar oíche ghar éigin,
Nuair luífid mo mhuinntir,
  Chun cainte le chéile.
Beidh mo dhá láimh ad thímcheall,
  Is mé ag innsint mo sgéil dhuit,
'S gurab é do chómhrá suairc mín tais
  Do bhain radharc fhlaithis Dé dhíom!

Tá an teine gan choigilt
  Is an solus gan mhúcha,
Tá an eochair faoi an ndorus,
  Is tarraing go ciúin í.
Tá mo mháthair 'n-a codla
  Agus mise im dhúiseacht,
Tá m'fhoirtiún im dhorn,
  Is mé ullamh chun siúil leat!

30. Máirín de Barra

A Mháirín de Barra, do mhairbh tú m'intinn,

I stretched out my hand to you,
  You pressed it with feeling,
I stayed with you then
  Till the lark's song came pealing!

That night – you remember? –
  We two were together
At the foot of the rowan tree
  While the night was freezing,
Your head on my bosom,
  Your bright pipe a-tuning,
'Twas little I thought then
  Of an end to our wooing!

Love of my heart within,
  Come some night soon,
– When my people are sleeping –
  That we may hold converse.
My arms will enfold you
  While I give you my message:
Your tender, gay, gentle speech
  Has robbed me of the sight of God's heaven!

Unraked is the fire,
  Still burning the light,
Beneath the door is the key,
  Draw it out quietly.
My mother is sleeping
  And I am keeping vigil,
My fortune's in my hand
  And I'm ready to go with you!

30. Máirín de Barra

This song, addressed to Máirín de Barra/ Maureen Barry, is one of the most impressive love lyrics in Modern Irish. The name de Barra is of Anglo-Norman origin. The last two lines of the poem have a vowel rhyme characteristic of the Irish of Ring, Co. Waterford.

Máirín de Barra, you have deadened my mind,

Is d'fhág tú beo dealabh mé gan fhios dom' mhuintir;
Ar mo luí dhom ar mo leabaidh is ort-sa bhím ag cuimhneamh,
'S ar m'éirí dhom ar maidin, mar do chealg tú an croí 'nam!

Do thugas 's do thugas 's do thugas óm chroí greann duit
Ar maidin lae'l Muire na gcoinneal sa teampall –
Do shúilín ba ghlaise ná uisce na ngeamhartha,
'S do bhéilín ba bhinne ná an druid nuair a labhrann.

Do shíl mé thú 'mhealladh le briathra 's le póga,
Do shíl mé thú 'mhealladh le leabhartha 's le móide,
Do shíl mé thú 'mhealladh ar bhreacadh na heornan,
Ach d'fhág tú dubhach dealabh ar theacht don mbliain nó mé.

Is aoibhinn don talamh a siúlann tú féin air,
Is aoibhinn don talamh nuair a sheinneann tú véarsa,
Is aoibhinn don leabaidh nuair a luíonn tú fé éadach,
'S is ró-aoibhinn don bhfear a gheobhaidh thú mar chéile.

Do shiúlóinn 's do shiúlóinn 's do shiúlóinn an saol leat,
Do rachainn tar sáile gan dá phingin spré leat;
Do thug mo chroí grá dhuit go brách brách ná tréigfidh,
'S go dtógfá ón mbás mé ach a rá gur leat féin mé.

A Mháirín, glac mo chomhairle 's ná seoltar tú ar t'aimhleas:
Seachain an stróinse, fear séite na hadhairce,
Gaibh leis an óigfhear 'na nglaonn siad Ó Floinn air –
Pós é de ghrá réitigh, ós é's toil le do mhuintir.

31. Bean an Fhir Rua

Tá siad dá rá
 Gur tú sáilín socair i mbróig,
Tá siad dá rá
 Gur tú béilín tana na bpóg.
Tá siad dá rá,
 'Mhíle grá dhil, go dtug tú dham cúl,
Cé go bhfuil fear le fáil,
 'S leis an táilliúirín bean an fhir ruaidh.

And left me in great distress, unknown to my kind,
When I lie down on my bed it's you I see before my eyes,
And how you pierce my heart, in the morning when I rise!

From the depths of my heart all my love to you I gave,
On that morning in the chapel at the Feast of the Presentation;
Brighter was your eye than dew on the green blades of corn,
And your mouth was sweeter than the voice of the starling.

I thought to beguile you with words and with kisses,
I thought to beguile you with books, with promises,
I thought to beguile you when the barley had ripened,
But you left me sad and dreary at the New Year's arrival.

Happy the ground where your own two feet tread,
Happy the ground when you're singing a verse,
Happy the bed when you lie under clothes,
And most happy for the man that will get you for his own!

I would walk, O I would walk with you the world wide,
I would cross the sea with you a penniless bride,
My heart gave you love that it never will forsake,
And you'd save me from death if myself you'd only take!

Máirín, do not be led astray, take my advice,
Beware of the stranger whose words can entice,
Take up with the young man they call O Flyne,
Marry him for peace' sake, as your people have in mind.

31. The Wife of the Red-Haired Man

This is one of the Modern Irish chansons d'amour *in which the woman
appears to be married, as in* amour courtois. *See Introduction, p. 19.*

> People do say:
>   Your little heel graces a shoe;
> People do say:
>   Your slender lips kiss well, too;
> People do say:
>   Thousand loves, that you've left me for life;
> Though there's a man you could take,
> It's the little tailor has the Red Man's wife.

Do thugas naoi mí
  I bpríosún ceangailte cruaidh,
Boltaí ar mo chaolaibh
  Is míle glas as súd suas.
Thúrfainn-se sidhe
  Mar thúrfadh eala cois cuain,
Le fonn do bheith sínte
  Síos le bean an fhir ruaidh.

Shaoil mise, a chéad-shearc,
  Go mbeadh aon-tigheas idir mé 's tú,
Shaoil mé 'n-a dhéidh sin
  Go mbréagfá mo leanbh ar do ghlúin.
Mallacht Rígh Neimhe
  Ar an té sin bhain dhíom-sa mo chlú,
Sin, agus uile go léir
  Lucht bréige chuir idir mé 's tú.

Tá crann ins an ngáirdín
  Ar a bhfásann duilliúr is bláth buí,
An uair leagaim mo lámh air
  Is láidir nach mbriseann mo chroí.
'Sé mo shólás go bás,
  Is é d'fháil ó fhlaitheas anuas,
Aon phóigín amháin,
  Is é d'fháil ó bhean an fhir ruaidh.

Ach go dtig lá an tsaoghail
  'N-a réabfar cnuic agus cuain,
Tiocfaidh smúit ar an ngréin
  'S beidh na néalta chomh dubh leis an ngual.
Beidh an fhairrge tirim,
  Is tiocfaidh na brónta 's na truaighe,
'S beidh an táilliúr a' sgreadach
  An lá sin faoi bhean an fhir ruaidh.

Nine months have I spent
   In prison closely tied,
Fetters on my wrists and ankles,
   On my body a thousand gyves.
I would soar
   Up like a swan o'er the tide,
Longing to lie
   With my darling the Red Man's wife.

I had thought, O my dear,
   That it's living together we'd be,
I thought after that
   You'd be coaxing my child on your knee.
The curse of Heaven's King
   On the one that my good name reviled,
And the tongues put a cloud between me
   And my darling the Red Man's wife.

There's a tree in the garden
   Grows green leaves and yellow bloom,
When I touch its bark with my hand
   It nearly breaks my heart.
'Tis my solace till death.
   To receive down from Heaven the delight
Of one kiss from the lips
   Of my darling the Red Man's wife.

And when that day comes
   That the hills and the havens are torn,
A veil o'er the sun,
   The clouds in the sky black as coal,
The sea will dry up,
   While sorrows and pities plague life,
And the tailor lament
   On that day for the Red Man's wife.

32. Mala Néifinn

Dá mbeinn-se ar mhala Néifinn
'S mo chéadghrá le mo thaoibh,
'S lách a chodlóimis in éineacht
Mar an t-éinín ar an gcraoibh;
'S é do bhéilín binn-bhréithreach
A mhéadaigh ar mo phian,
'S codladh ciúin ní fhéadaim
Go n-éagad, fairíor!

Dá mbeinn-se ar na cuanta
Mar ba dhual dom, gheobhainn spórt,
Mo chairde uilig faoi bhuaireamh
'S gruaim orthu gach ló;
Fíorscoth na ngruagach
Fuair bua ins gach gleo,
Mo chroí istigh tá ina ghual dubh
'S bean mo thruaí níl beo.

Nach aoibhinn do na héiníní
Éiríos go hard,
'S chodlaíos in éineacht
Ar aon chraeibhín amháin,
Ní hé sin dom féineach
'S dom chéad míle grá,
Is fada fánach óna chéile
Bhíos ár n-éirí gach lá.

Nuair a fhosclas na spéartha
Is éiríos an lá,
Tá'n lán mara 'na dhéidh sin
Ag dul in aghaidh srutha ag trá.
Mar siúd bhíos an té úd
Bheir an-toil don ghrá –
Mar chrann ar mhala shléibhe
Ina dtréigfeadh a bhláth.

32. The Brow of Nephin

Although the scene of this song is west Mayo, Douglas Hyde, who included it in his Love Songs of Connacht, *heard part of it from a woman in Roscommon.*

Were I on the brow of Nephin
And my first love there with me,
We would sleep nestling together
Like songbirds on a tree.
Your dear lips sweetly speaking
That has increased my pain,
I cannot sleep in peace, alas,
Until my dying day!

If I were sailing round the bays,
As I should be, I'd have sport,
With all my friends disconsolate,
Their spirits ever low;
A champion without parallel,
Victorious in every fight,
My heart within to black ash turned,
No woman to pity my plight.

How happy for the little birds
That soar aloft so high,
And sleep together
On the one little bough.
This happiness is not for me
And the one love of my life:
Far distant from each other
Each morning when we rise.

When the skies have brightened
And the day has cleared,
After that the high tide
Ebbs against the stream.
So fares the person
Whom love can so consume,
Like a tree on the mountain side
Forsaken by its bloom.

33. An Seanduine

Is triúr a bhí agam am cheangal le h-iarlais,
Mo mháthair is mh'athair is a' sagart chomh dian leo:
Chuadar abhaile 's do chaitheadar féasta,
'S is annamh a thigeann mo charaid 'om fhéachaint.

Is óró a sheanduine, leat-sa ní gheód-sa,
Is óró a sheanduine, leat-sa ní gheód-sa,
Óró a sheanduine, leat-sa ní gheód-sa,
'S is mór a' trua an chríonnacht a' claoi leis an óige !

Comhairle 'sea fuaireas amuh ar a' mbóthar
Ó rógaire sagairt an seanduine 'phósa;
Ba chuma leis é ach go méadóinn a phócaí,
'S mé bheith fad a mhairfinn a' braith ar na comharsain.

Phós mise an seanduine, bhí orm díth céille,
Rinne mé an méid sin ar chomhairle mo ghaolta;
Chuaidh mé abhaile leis – fó-ríor an sgéal san!
Is d'éirigh mé ar maidin is b'fhearr liom an t-éag dom.

Dá bhfaghainn-se mo sheanduine báite i bpoll móna,
Thúrfainn abhaile é 's do dhéanfainn é 'thórramh,
Chuirfinn glas ar a' ndorus is an eochair im póca,
'S do shiúlóinn amach leis na buachaillíbh óga.

'S dá mbeadh súd agam-sa, capall is srian air,
Iallait mhaith leathair 'gus béalbhach iarainn,
Bhéarfainn mo sheanduine amach ins a' tsliabh liom,
'Gus do thúrfainn a' faraire abhaile ins an iallait.

Do chuas-sa go Corcaigh a d'iarraidh gléas tórraimh,
Tobac agus snaois agus cláracha cómhran:
Ar theacht dom abhaile go tuirseach tinn brónach,
Cé gheóinn ach mo sheanduine 'róstáil bruthóige!

'Twas plain to see she'd rather die,
Tears streamed without easing from her eyes,
And she straight as an arrow in the centre of the stand,
Pressing her fingers and wringing her hands.
When she had wept great floods of tears
And her sighs released the sounds of her speech,
Her gloom passed off, her complexion cleared,
She dried her face and her words were these:

b) *She Speaks for the Unmarried Girls (167-190)*

'A thousand welcomes, may joy await thee,
Venerable seeress, Eeval, from Craglee!
O bright light of day, most august lady,
O worldly treasure in a prison of dearth,
O victorious leader from the joyous hosts[3]
You are sorely needed in Thomond and Ireland.
The reason of my anguish, the cause of my grievance,
The matter that has vexed me and left me defeated,
In disarray and without right reason,
Cast like mist in burning pain:
The throngs, the flower and pick of ladies
Left in this world unwed, uncared for,
Spinsters without spouse to cherish them,
Discarded unpraised, without taint of evil.
I know myself in the places I've travelled
A hundred and one who wouldn't refuse
– And I too, alas, am in like case –
Without husband or child, left barren and useless.
Alas for the pain and grief that we feel,
Without vantage or wealth or peace or ease,
Gloomy and sad, in toil and need,
Without rest or love commerce or sleep,
But harrowed by care, without peace or leisure,
A prey to our thoughts on a bed without pleasure!

c) *Behaviour Of the Men (191-226)*

O chaste one of Crag, observe with attention
The women of Ireland in tribulation,
So that if the men persist in their course,
Alas! we women must take them by force.

'Sé am ar mhéin leo céile a phósadh
An t-am nár mhéin le héinne góil leo,
An t-am nárbh fhiú bheith fúthu sínte
– Seandaigh thamhanda shúite chloíte!
Dá dtiteadh amach le teas na hóige
Duine fén seacht ar theacht féasóige   200
Ceangal le mnaoi, ní míntais thoghfaidh,
Taithneamhach shuíte de shíol ná d'fhoghluim,
Clódheas chaoin ná míonla mhánla,
Arb eol di suí nó tíocht do láthair,
Ach doineantach odhar nó donn doilíosach
Chruinnigh le doghraing cabhair nár chuí dhi!
'Sé chráigh mo chroí is do scaoil gan chéill mé
Is d'fhág mo smaointe is m'intinn traochta,
Tráite tinn mar taoim go tréithlag,
Cásmhar claoite ag caoi 's ag géarghol: 210
An uair chím preabaire calma croíúil
Fuadrach fearamhail barramhail bríomhar…
Nó buachaill bastalach beachanta brógdheas
Cruacheart ceannasach ceaptha córach
– Buaite ceannaithe ceangailte pósta
Ag fuaid, ag cailligh, ag aimid nó ag óinmhid,
Nó ag suairle salach de chaile gan tionscal,
Stuaiceach stailceach aithiseach stúncach   220
Suaiteach sotalach focalach fáigiúil
Cuairdeach codlatach goirgeach gráiniúil.
Mo chreach is mo lot! Tá molt míbhéasach,
Caile-na-gcos-is-folt-gan-réiteach,
Dá ceangal anocht, 'sé loisc go léir mé,
Is ca bhfuil mo locht ná toghfaí raeimpi?

Créad é an t-abhar ná tabharfaí grá dhom
Is mé chomh leabhair, comh modhamhail, chomh breá so?
Is deas mo bhéal, mo dhéad 's mo gháire,
Is deas mo ghné, is tá m'éadan tláth tais,   230
Is glas mo shúil, tá m'úrla scáinneach
Bachallach búclach cúplach fáinneach,
Mo leaca is mo ghnúis gan smúid gan smáchaill,
Tarraingthe cúmtha lonrach scáfar,
Mo phíob, mo bhráid, mo lámha 's mo mhéire

The time they're willing to marry a wife
Is the time that no one would want to unite with them,
When it's no longer worth while to lie beneath them
– Sapless old men worn out and unwieldly.
If in the heat of youth it fell out
To one in seven when the beard did first sprout
To marry, he'd pick no mild gentle maiden,
Agreeable, staid, well-born, educated,
Of polished mien, gentle and pleasant,
Who knew how to sit and had a good presence,
But a sallow wintry crone or a rueful brown hag,
Who in hardship her ill-suited wealth had gathered.
What has vexed my heart and driven me daft,
Left my thoughts and my mind exhausted,
Drained and ill as I am, depleted,
Lamenting, oppressed and bitterly weeping,
When I see a gallous lad hearty and strong
Active, manly, humorous, vigorous...[4]
Or a well-shod, lively, dashing blade,
Sturdy and masterful, sociable, well-made,
Captured and bought and in marriage bound
To a wretch, a hag, a fool or a clown,
Or to a dirty lump of a witless wench,
Abusive, sulky, stubborn, sullen,
Disturbing, arrogant, wordy, a scolder,
Rambling, sleepy, surly, odious.
Woe and alas! There's an impudent hussy
With feet like ploughs and hair in tussocks
To be married this night, it has scalded me sorely,
For why shouldn't I be picked before her?

d) *Her Charms: Self-Portrait (227-246)*

Why shouldn't I be the object of yearning,
And I so slender, so graceful and charming?
Comely my lips, my teeth, my smile,
My features and face are gentle and mild;
My eyes are grey, my forelock pleated,
In ringlets and double-plaits, coiled so neatly,
My cheek and my face without blot or blemish,
Etched and shapely, shining and comely,
My throat and neck, my fingers and hands,

Ag síorbhreith barr na háille ó chéile.
Féach mo chom! Nach leabhair mo chnámha!
Níl mé lom ná crom ná stágach,
Seo toll is cosa agus colainn nach nár dom,
Is an togha go socair fá cover ná tráchtaim. 240
Ní suairle caile ná sreangaire mná mé,
Ach stuaire cailce tá taithneamhach breá deas;
Ní sraoill ná sluid ná luid gan fáscadh
Ná smíste duirc gan sult gan sásamh,
Lóiste lofa ná toice gan éifeacht
Ach ógbhean scofa chomh tofa 's is féidir.

Dá mbeinnse silte, mar thuille dem chomharsain,
Leadhbach liosta, gan tuiscint gan eolas,
Gan radharc gan ghliocas in imirt mo chórach,
Mo threighid! Cár mhiste mé rith in éadóchas! 250
Ní fhacathas fós mé i gcóngar daoine
Ag faire nó ag tórramh óg ná críonna,
Ar mhachaire an bháire, an ráis ná an rince,
I bhfarradh na dtáinte ar bhánta líonta
Ach gofa go sámh gan cháim ar domhan
I gculaithe sásta ó bharr go bonn:
Beidh a cheart im chúl de phúdar fillte,
Starch is stiúir i gcúl mo chaidhpe,
Húda geal gan cheal ribíní,
Gúna breac 's a cheart rufaí leis; 260
Is annamh go brách gan fásáil aerach
Taithneamhach breá lem' cheárdán craorag,
Is an-iomú luíonna, craíocha is éanlaith
Im aparún síogach ríogach cambric;
Sála cúmtha cúnga córach'
Arda sleamhaine ar scriú fém bróga;
Búclaí is fáinní is láimhní síoda,
Fonsaí, práslaí is lásaí daora.

Seachain, ná síl gur scínteach scáfar,
Aimid gan ghaois ná naíonach náireach 270
Eaglach uaigneach uallach fhiain mé,

Each more beautiful than the other.
See my waist! How slender my bones!
I'm not bare or bent or clumsy.
Of thighs, legs and body I'm not ashamed,
All of the best dressed in clothes I'll not name.
I'm no slut of a woman, no gangling haverel,
But beautiful, young, pleasant and graceful;
No shapeless lump, no ragged sloven,
No cheerless boor unused to comfort,
No lazy lounger, no useless jade,
But a lively young woman, as fine as they're made.

e) *Her Dress (247-268)*

If I were inept, like some of my neighbours,
Untidy, sluggish, without knowledge or sense,
Without vision or cunning in getting fair play,
Why, then, small loss if I were to despair!
I've never been seen yet where people meet,
At vigil or wake of the old or the young,
On the field of play, at race or at dance,
Where crowds foregather in close-packed fields,
But from top to bottom I was faultlessly dressed
In agreeable, well-fitting clothes of the best.
To my hair was applied its share of powder,
My coif at the back starched and slanted,
A white hood with no lack of ribbons,
A speckled gown with its share of ruffs on it.
'Twas seldom my scarlet hood and cloak
Were without fine bright airy facings,
Herbs and branches and birds in great numbers
On my striped and patterned cambric apron;
Handsome, shapely, smooth, narrow heels
Set high on screws on my shoes beneath,
Buckles and rings and bracelets,
Silk gloves, fillets and expensive laces.

f) *Her Social Life (269-286)*

Mind you, don't think I'm timid or flighty,
A green young fool or a bashful babe,
Fearful, lonely, haughty or wild,

Gealtach gan ghuais gan stuaim gan téagar –
I bhfalach ní raghainnse ó radharc na gcéata,
Is ceannasach taibhseach m'aghaidh is m'éadan.
Is dearfa bhím am shíorthaspánadh
Ar mhachaire mhín gach fíoriomána,
Ag rínce, báire, rás is radaireacht,
Tínte cnámh is ráfla is ragairne,
Aonach, margadh is Aifreann Domhnaigh
Ag éileamh breathnaithe, ag amharc 's ag togha fir.   280
Chaitheas mo chiall le fiach gan éifeacht,
Dhalladar riamh mé, is d'iadar m'ae ionnam,
Tréis mo chumainn, mo thurraing 's mo ghrá dhóibh,
Tréis ar fhulaing mé d'iomada cránais,
Tréis ar chaitheas le caitheamh na scálaí,
Béithe balbha, is cailleacha cártaí.

Níl cleas dá mbéidir léamh ná trácht air
Le teacht na ré nó tréis bheith lán di,
Um Inid, um Shamhain, ná ar shiúl na bliana
Ná tuigim gur leamhas bheith ag súil le ciall as!   290
Níorbh áil liom codladh go socair aon uair díobh
Gan lán mo stoca de thorthaibh fém chluasa,
Is deimhin nárbh obair liom troscadh le cráifeacht,
Is greim ná blogam ní shlogainn trí trátha;
In aghaidh na srotha do thomainn mo léine
Ag súil trím chodladh le cogar óm chéile;
Is minic do chuaigh mé ag scuabadh ón stáca,
M'ingne is gruaig fán luaithghríos d'fhágainn,
Chuirinn an tsúist fá chúl na gaibhle,
Chuirinn an ramhan go ciúin fán adhart chúm,   300
Chuirinn mo choigeall i gcillín na hátha,
Chuirinn mo cheirtlín i dtiníl Rághnaill,
Chuirinn an ros ar chorp na sráide,
Chuirinn sa tsop fúm tor gabáiste.
Níl cleas acu súd dá ndúras láithreach
Ná hagrainn cúnamh an Deamhain 's a bhráithre!
'Sé fáth mo scéil go léir 's a bhrí dhuit
– Táim gan chéile tréis mo dhíchill,
Fáth mo sheanchas fhada, mo phian-chreach!
Táim in achrann daingean na mblianta,   310

Without push or substance, skittish, unstable.
No way would I hide from the eye of the people,
Noble and splendid my face and appearance,
'Tis certain I'm always on display
On the level field of each true hurling game.
At dancing, football, races and outings,
At bonfires, gossipings, late carousals,
At mass on Sunday, at fair and market,
Wooing the eye, viewing and picking men.
I've expended my wit in vain pursuit,
They've blinded me ever and broken my heart,
After all my companionship, dash and affection,
After all I've suffered of pain and affliction,
After all I've lost when the cups went spinning[5]
With mumbling fortune-tellers and card-reading women.

g) *The Pishogues[6] She Practises (287-312)*

Of all the tricks you can read or speak of
At the waxing moon or when it is waning,
At Shrovetide, Hollantide, during the year,
I know none but it's foolish to expect any meaning from.
I wouldn't sleep calmly at times such as these
Without a stockingful of fruit under my ears.
It gave me no trouble to fast with devotion
And no bite or sup would I swallow all day.
I'd dip my shift against the running stream
Hoping my husband would whisper through my sleep.
I often went sweeping from the stack of hay,
On the embers I'd leave bits of nail and hair.
In the corner of the hearth-ope I'd put the flail,
Under the pillow I'd settle the spade,
In the kiln near the ford my distaff would go,
In Reynolds' limekiln my clew I'd throw,
The hayseed I'd leave on the middle of the street,
And the head of cabbage in the straw of my bed.
With every trick that I've mentioned now
I'd call the devil and his brethren to help me out.
The cause of my tale and its meaning is this:
I'm without a husband in spite of my best.
My long story's motive, my pain and my woe!:
I'm tightly caught in the moving years,

Ag tarraing go tréan ar laethaibh liatha,
Is eagal liom éag gan éinne am iarraidh.

Is fada gan feidhm is foidhne dhómhsa é,
Lagar am leaghadh, agus leigheas im chomhachta
Maille le luíonna díbhlí dreoite
Is arthanna draíochta chloífeas fós dom
Buachaill deas nó gas galánta
Is bhuaifeas ceart a shearc 's a ghrá dhom.
Ch'naic mé go leor den tsórt so á dhéanamh
Is chuirfinn i gcóir na cóngair chéanna:
Is daingean an cúnamh ag dúbailt daoine
Greamanna d'úlla is púdar luíonna,   340
Magairlín meidhreach, meill na mbualtaibh,
Taithigín taibhseach, toill na tuairte,
Mealladh na mínnseach, claíomh na mbonsach,
An cuiminín buí, 's a ndraíocht chun drúise;
Duilliúr dóite ar nós gur rún é,
Is tuille den tsórt nach cóir é mhúineadh.
B'iongantas muar i dTuain le chéile
An bhruinneal so thuas ag buachaint céile,
Is d'inis sí dómhsa – ar ndó trí rún –
Um Inid, 's í pósta ó bhord na Samhan,   350
Nár ith 's nár ól an fóntach fionn
Ach cuile na móna dóite ar lionn.
Is fada mé ag foighne, faghaimse fuascailt,
Seachain ar mhoill mé, saighid chun luais é;
Mura bhfuil leigheas dom threighid id chuairdse
Cuirfidh mé faghairt i bhfeidhm, más crua dhom.'

Travelling quickly towards grey old age,
I fear I will die unwed, an old maid.

*In the next eighteen lines she beseeches Eeval to save her from the fate of an
old maid – and from the mockery of successful rivals. Otherwise she will resort
to drastic measures:*

h) *Herbs for Husbands (331-356)*

I've long to no end in patience endured,
Consumed by weakness – within reach of a cure
From common herbs and they withered to dust
And magic charms I know I can trust
To win a bold blade or a pleasing lad
And assure me his love and tender regard.
I saw a lot of these being made
And I would prepare the very same.
For yoking couples, reliable means
Are fragments of apples and dust of herbs,
The early purple orchid, the cowslip,
The knotted figwort and the toadstool,
The goat's beard, the grass plantain,
The cummin seed, with their sexual potence;
Foliage burnt where no eye can see,
And more of the kind that I oughtn't reveal.[7]
All Thomand was shocked when the girl here above
Succeeded in bringing her man to the altar;
'Twas myself she told – of course, in secret –
At Shrove and she married since Hallowe'en:
His only provision before him at table
Was gnats from the bog and they burnt on ale.
Long have I borne it, 'tis time I was freed,
Further delay will launch me at speed:
Unless from your visit my pain can be cured,
If I am hard pressed, I'll appeal to the sword.'

II

Preabann anuas go fuadrach fíochmhar
Seanduine suarach is fuadach nimhe fé,
A bhaill ar luascadh is luas anáile air,
Dradhain is duais ar fuaid a chnámha,   360
Ba d'reoil an radharc go deimhin don chúirt é,
Ar bhord na taibhse im eisteacht dúirt sé:–

'Dochar is díobháil is síorchrá cléibh ort,
A thoice le míostá 'e shíol gá is déirce!
Is dóch nach iongantas laigeacht na gréine
Is fós gach tubaist dár imigh ar Éire,
Mar mheath gach ceart gan reacht gan dlí againn,
Ár mba a bhí bleacht gan lacht gan laoigh acu...

Is fíor gur feasach mé farairí Fódla
Suíte greamaithe ag sladairí 'en tsórt so.   430
Dar lámh mo charad! Is aithnid dom comharsa
Láimh le baile againn, gairid do chóngar,
Buachaill soineanta, sruimile sóntach,
– Buaileadh duine acu chuige mar nóchar.
Is searbh lem chroí, nuair chím im radharc í,
A gradam, a críoch, a poimp 's a taibhse,
Sealbhach bó aici 's eorna ag fás di,
Airgead póca is ór idir lámha aici.
Chonaic mé inné í ar thaobh na sráide,
Is cumasach tréan an léire mná í!   440
Malfaire másach mágach magúil,
Marbh le cámas, lán de ladús;

Part II. Case for the Defence

a) *The Advocate: A Pen-Picture (357-362)*

Then a wretched old man bounced down to the table
Lively and fierce and in venomous haste,
His limbs ajig and he gasping sore,
Stiffness and pain in all his bones.
A miserable sight to the court, indeed,
As he stood at the bench and began to plead:

b) *His Counter-Attack (363-428)*

'Harm and loss on you! – and lasting grief!
You sarcastic hussy, born of alms and need!
It is surely no wonder the sunlight is veiled,
Or misfortune dogs the land of Erin,
If our rights are all gone, without rule or law,
Our cows that were milking gone sterile and dry...

*He continues in this vein in a personal and scurrilous attack on the girl and
her relatives; not only are they destitute, but her fine outfit was acquired
dubiously, he insinuates. Then, turning to the fairy queen Eeval, he offers this
exemplum:*

c) *How the Men are Duped: Predicament of
a Neighbour (429-476)*

I know indeed that the brave lads of Ireland
Are caught in the toils of rogues of this kind.
By the hand of my friend! A neighbour I know,
From beside our home, just a stone's throw,
An innocent lad, a guileless poor fellow,
Happened to take one of these for a wife.
My heart misgives me when I see her before me,
Her airs and graces, her pride and her showing,
With her herd of cows and her barley growing,
Money in pocket and she handling gold.
I saw her yesterday on the side of the street,
Tall, strong and well-built, as fine as you'd meet,
Sturdy and broad-hipped, plump and jeering,
Proud as a peacock, silly and wheedling;

Marach gur claon liom éad a mhúscailt,
Scannal a scé', ná scéalta a scrúdadh,
B'fhuras dom ínsint cruinn mar chuala
An chuma 'na mbíodh sí sraoilte suaite
Stractha ar lár, is gáir 'na timpeall,
Caite ar an sráid, nó i stábla sínte.
Mairfidh a tásc, is tráchtfar choíche
Ar mharana, ar cháil, ar gháir a gníomhartha   450
In Íbh Breacáin an aráin 's an fhíona,
I dTír Mhic Calláin na mbánta míne,
Ag ísle is árda Bháinse is Inse,
Chill Bhreacáin, an Chláir is Chuínche,
Ag consaigh ainigí Thradraí an phónra
Is fionsaigh fhalachaí Chreatalaí an chórda.

Faire! Ba claon í; tréis a ndúirt mé,
Ghlacfainn gur saor í fána cionta,
Ach bheirim don phláigh í, lá mar chínn í,
Leagtha láimh le Gárus, sínte   460
Caite ar an ród gan órlach fúithi
Ag gramaisc na móna ar bhóithribh Dhubhdhoire.
M'iongantas ann ós ceann mo chéille
– Is crithim go fann le scanradh an scéil seo –
Ise bheith seang nuair theann gach éinne í,
Is druidim le clann nuair shantaigh féin é!
Is mór na grásta é rá na mbriathra:
Nóimint spáis níor ghá le hiarraidh
Ó léadh ar bord di os comhair na gcoínnle
An tEgo Vos so d'ordaigh Íosa   470
Gur shéid sí lacht go bleacht 'na cíochaibh
Ach nao' mí beacht is seachtain chinnte!
Breathain gur baol don té tá scaoilte
Ceangal go héag fá thaobh den chuing seo
I sealbh gach saoth, is éad á shuathadh
– In aisce, mo léan, mo léann ní bhfuair mé.

Is feasach don taobh so den tsaol mar bhí mé
Sealad dem réim is dem laethaibh roímhe seo,
Leitheadach láidir, lán de shaidhbhreas,
Eisteas le fáil is fáilte im theaghlach,   480

But that I think it wicked to cause jealous feelings,
Giving out scandal or prying into tales,
I could easily tell it just as I heard it,
The way she used to be dragged and shaken,
Pulled to the ground with an outcry round her,
Thrown on the street or stretched in a stable.
Her tidings will live and the story be told
Of the fame, the report, the repute of her deeds
In Ibrickan of the bread and the wine,
In Teermaclane of the level fields,
Among gentle and simple of Ennis and Bansha,
And of Kilbracken, Clare and Quin;
Among the wicked bounders of Tradree-the-Beans
And the cowardly swindlers of Cratloe-the-Cord.

Alas! She was wicked; after all I've said
I'd take her as innocent of her crimes,
If I didn't see her – a plague on her kind! –
Stretched on the ground near Garus lying,
Thrown on the road without a shred beneath
By the moorland rabble on the Doora streets.
I'm lost in wonderment, I cannot explain,
– I quiver in weakness with the fright of the tale –
She remained slender while everyone squeezed her,
And was got with child just when it pleased her!
Great is the grace in the sacred words:
She never needed a moment's respite
When the Ego Vos that Jesus prescribed
Was read aloud under candlelight
But nine months neat and one week just
To sluice the milk to her swelling bust!
See what peril to the man who is free
To be tied for life in a yoke of the kind,
A prey to all torments, to jealousy!
– Alas! My knowledge has cost me dear.

d) *His Own Marriage (477-532)*

My story is known to the countryside,
How in earlier days for a space of time
I was proud and rich and full of wealth,
With a house of welcome for passers-by,

Caraid i gcúirt is cúnamh dlí agam,
Ceannas is clú is comhar na saoithe,
Tathag im chaínt is suím is éifeacht,
Talamh is maoin ag suíomh mo chéille,
M'aigne síoch agus m'íntinn sásta:
Chailleas le mnaoi mo bhrí is mo shláinte!

Ba taithneamhach leabhair an crobhaire mná í,
Bhí seasamh is com is cabhail is cnámha aici;
Casadh 'na cúl go búclach trilseach,
Lasadh 'na gnúis go lonrach soilseach,   490
Cuma na hóige uirthi is só 'na gáire,
Is cuireadh 'na cló chun póg is fáilte.
Och! Chreathas le fonn gan chonn gan cháirde
Ó bhaitheas go bonn go tabhartha-i-ngrá dhi.
Is dearbh gan dabht ar domhan gur díoltas
Danartha donn dom thabhairt ar m'aímhleas
D'fhearthainn go trom ar bhonn mo ghníomhartha
Ó Fhlaitheas le fonn do lom 'na líon mé.

Do snamanadh suíte snaídhm na cléire
Is ceangaladh sínn í gcuíng le chéile,   500
Ghlanas gan chinnteacht suím gach éilimh
Bhaineas le baois-gan-ghaois an lae sin.
Cothrom go leor, níor chóir mé cháineadh,
Stopas an gleo bhí ag cóip na sráide
– Bacaigh go léir – bhí an cléireach sásta,
An sagart ró-bhaoch (is béidir fáth leis!)
Lasamair tóirse is comharsain cruínn ann,
Leagadh ar bórdaibh mórchuid bídh chúinn;
Clagarnach cheoil is ól gan choímse,
Is chaitheadar cóisir mhórtach mhaíteach.   510

Mo dhíth gan easpa nár tachtadh le bia mé
An oíche baisteadh nó as sin gur iarr mé
Síneadh ar leabain le hainnir do liaith mé
Is scaoil le gealaigh gan charaid gan chiall mé!
Sé tásc do gheobhainn ag óg 's ag aosta
Gur breallán spóirt ag ól 's ag glaoch í,
I mbotháin ósta is bóird á bpléasgadh
Ar lár 'na lóiste ag pósta is aonta.
B'fhada á mheilt a teist 's a tuairisc,

Friends at court and legal advice,
Power and fame and the ear of the wise.
My comments had substance and value and force,
Land and property bearing them witness;
My spirit at rest and my mind content,
With a woman I lost my health and my strength!

Delightful, slender and sturdy was she,
With her stance and waist and body and bones;
Her ringleted hair in tresses and twists,
With a fine animation her face was lit;
She looked so young, with such joy in her smile,
Her facial expression a kiss did invite.
O, I quivered with longing from head to heels,
In instant love, bereft of reason.
It's sure and certain it was Heaven's vengeance,
Terrible, deadly, bringing me ruin,
Heavily poured down for the sins of my life
That swept me into its net in delight.

The clergy's knot was fastened and bound,
And there we were married, safe and sound;
Without counting the cost, all the bills I paid
Which are part of the extravagant folly of the day.
Fair enough, I shouldn't be blamed;
I put a stop to the noise of the rabble rout
– Street beggars all – the cleric was pleased,
And the priest much beholden (now what was the reason?)
The neighbours were gathered, the torch we kindled,
Food was piled on the tables unstinted,
While the music cascaded and drink flowed free,
They partook of a splendid, spectacular feast.

My ruin, complete! – that my food didn't choke me
On the night of my baptism, or from then to the night
I lay with the girl who has darkened my life,
And driven me distracted without friend or guidance.
The word I got from the young and the old was
That she was a laughing stock drinking and toasting
In shebeens where tables were crashing,
Stretched on the floor with single and married.
Her fame and repute were long being consumed,

B'fhada gur chreid mé a bheag nó a mhuar de;   520
Dob eaglach le gach beirt dá gcuala é
Go rachainn im peilt im gheilt gan tuairisc.

Fós ní ghéillfinn, caoch mar bhí mé,
Do ghlór-gan-éifeacht éinne mhaígh é,
Ach magadh nó greim-gan-feidhm gan chéill
– Gur aithris a broinn dom deimhin gach scéil!
Níor chúrsaí leamhais ná dúrdam bréige é,
Dúirt-bean-liúm-go-ndúirt-bean-léi é,
Ach labhair an bheart i gceart 's in éifeacht:
Bhronn sí mac i bhfad roimh ré orm;   530
Mo scanradh sceil! gan féith dem chroí air,
Clann dá dtéamh dom tréis na hoíche!

Callóid anfach ainigí scólta,
Bunóc ceangailte is bean an tí breoite,
Posóid leagtha ar smeachaidí teo acu,
Is cuinneog bhainne á greadadh le fórsa,
Is mullach ar lánmhias bánbhia is siúicre
Ag Murainn Ní Cháimlia, bán-lia an chrúca!
Bhí coiste cruinnithe ag tuille dem chomharsain
Cois na tine, agus siosarnach dómhsa,   540
Scaoilid cogar i bhfogas dom eisteacht:
'Míle moladh le Solas na Soilse!
Bíodh nach baileach a d'aibigh an chré seo,
Chímse an t-athair 'na sheasamh 'na chéadfa!
A bhfeiceann tú, a Shadhbh 'rú, loigheamh a ghéaga,
A dheilbh gan droinn, a bhaill 's a mhéara,
Cumas na lámh ba dána dóirne,
Cuma na gcnámh is fás na feola?'
Cheapadar cruinn gur shíolra' an dúchas
Maise mo ghnaoi agus íor mo ghnúise,   550
Feilleadh mo shrón is lónradh m'éadain,
Deiseacht mo chló, mo shnó is m'fhéachaint,
Leagadh mo shúl is fiú mo gháire
– Is as sin do shiúil ó chúl go sála é!
Amharc ná radharc ní bhfaighinn den chréice,
"Is baileach gan leigheas do mhillfeadh gaoth é,"
– Ag cuideachta an teaghlaigh i bhfeighil mo chaochta –
"Siolla dá laghad di leaghfa' an créatúir!"

'Twas long till I credited little or much of it.
Every two who heard the tale
Feared I'd rush off, stone mad and stark naked.

I still wouldn't believe – I was so blind –
The babbling voice of any who told it,
'Twas a jibe or a joke without point or sense
– Till her arching stomach made everything clear.
'Twas no trifling jest or lying tale,
The echo of rumour by women regaled,
But the fact was plain as the sun in the sky:
She bore me a son long before her time.
Frightful to tell! No inkling had I
Of family being warmed for me after the night!

e) *The Illegitimate Baby (533-558)*

A stormy commotion, furious, raging,
The infant swaddled, the mother still ailing,
A warm drink set over heated embers,
And a churn of milk being stirred with energy.
The covetous female assistant was heaping
The piled platter with sugar and white meats![8]
The committee gathered by some of my neighbours
Were at the fireside whispering designedly towards me.
They launched a murmur within range of my ear:
'A thousand praises to the Light of Lights!
Although the babe is not yet fully ripe,
I see the father again in his looks.
Sive, do you see the lie of his members,
His straight-backed frame, his limbs and fingers,
The power of his hands with their mettlesome fists,
The form of his bones and the growth of the flesh?'
They thought precisely that nature had bred
My beauty of feature, the shape of my visage,
The turn of my nose, the gleam of my face,
My elegant form, complexion and glance,
The set of my eyes and even my smile
– And all the way down from my head to my heels.
Sight nor light could I get of the infant,
"The wind would devastate him completely,"
– Said the household company bent on deceiving me –
"The slightest draught of it would melt the creature!"

Do labhras garg is d'agaras Íosa,
Is stollta garbh do bhagaras gríosach,   560
D'fhógaras fearg le hainbhios caínte;
Is dóch gur chreathadar cailleacha an tí romham,
Ar leisce an achrainn leagadar chúm é:
"Beir go haireach air, seachain ná brúigh é,
Is furas é shuathadh, luaisc go réidh é
– Turraing do fuair sí a ruaig roimh ré é –
Seachain ná fáisc é, fág 'na loighe é,
Is gairid an bás do, is gearr a ragha' sé,
Is dá maireadh go lá idir lámha 'na chló,
'S an sagart ar fáil, níorbh fhearr a bheith beo!"   570
Do bhaineas an tsnaídhm dá chuibhreach cumhdaigh,
Bhreathain mé cruinn é sínte ar ghlún liom;
Ambuaireach, d'airigh mé tathagach teann é,
Fuair mé feargach fearsadach lúfach
Láidir leathan mo leanbh 'na ghuaille,
Sála daingeana is ana-chuid gruaige air,
Cluasa cruinnithe is inginí fásta;
Chruadar a uilleanna, a chroibh is a chnámha,
D'aibigh a shúile, is fiú a pholláirí,
Is d'airigh mé a ghlúine lúfar láidir,   580
– Coileán cumasach cuisleannach córach
Folláin fuilingeach fuinneamhach feolmhar!

Screadaim go hard le gáir na tíre
Is leagaim dod láthair cás na ndaoine;
Breathain go caoin, is bí truamhéileach,
Beannaibh a gcinn is suím a gcéille!
Athraigh an dlí seo, cuing na cléire,
Is ainic an bhuíon nár fríoth sa ngéibheann.
Má lagaigh an síolrach díonmhar daonna
I dtalamh dathaoibhinn fhíorghlas Éireann,   590
Is furas an tír d'aithlíonadh de laochaibh
D'uireasa a nguí gan bhrí gan éifeacht.
Cá bhfuil an gá le gáir na bainse,
Cárta biotáille is pá lucht seinnte,
Sumaigh ar bórd go fóiseach taibhseach,

f) *The Baby is Examined (559-582)*

Roughly I spoke out and called on Jesus,
Fiercely and loudly I threatened the *greesa.*[9]
I displayed my anger with reckless speeching,
No doubt the old women shivered in fear of me;
They wanted no quarrel and handed him over,
"Take him up carefully, make sure you don't press,
He's easy upset, rock him gently,
– A fall she got that brought him on early –
Take care would you squeeze him, leave him lying,
He's barely in it, he's near to dying.
If he lasts out till dawn in hands as he is,
And the priest is by – sure that's better than living!"
I loosened the knot of his swaddling cloth,
Closely I studied him stretched on my knee;
By the mass! I found him solid and strong,
Lusty, lively with sinew and brawn;
The child had shoulders strong and wide,
Firm heels and plenty of hair,
Well-set ears and nails well-grown,
Solid elbows, hands and bones,
His eyes and his nostrils were well-formed,
His knees were lively and strong, I found,
– A powerful, strong-limbed, shapely baby,
Healthy and plump, vigorous and hardy!

g) *The Case for Natural Love (583-606)*

I cry aloud the country's case
And place before you the people's plaint:
Consider with sympathy, view with compassion
Their horns of jealousy,[10] the sum of their sense.
Change this law, the yoke of the clerics
And save all those not yet in fetters.
If the kindly human seed is impaired
In pleasant, colourful, verdant Erin,
Renewal of stalwarts can easily take place
Without their senseless and useless prayer.
Where is the need for the wedding commotion,
Quarts of whiskey, paying musicians,
Striplings disporting, wanton and showy,

179

Gliogar is gleo acu, is ól á saighdeadh,
Ó d'aibigh an t-abhar do bhronn Mac Dé
Gan sagart ar domhan á dtabhairt dá chéile?
Is leathanmhar láidir lánmhar léadmhar
Fairsing le fáil an t-álmhach saor so.   600
Is minic do chímse bríomhar bórrtha
Cumasach líonta i gcroí 's i gcóir iad,
Créim ní fheicim ná daille ná caoiche
I léim-ar-leithre dár hoileadh ó mhnaoi ar bith;
Is mó 's is mire 's is teinne 's is tréine
A gcló 's a gclisteacht ná dlisteanaigh éinne!

Is fuiris a luaimse d'fhuascailt suíte
Is duine acu an uair seo ar fuaid an tí seo.
An bhfeiceann tú thall go ceansa ciúin é?
Deisigh anall i dteannta an bhúird é,   610
Breathain go cruinn é; bíodh gurb og é,
Is dearfa suíte an píosa feola é,
Is preabaire i dtoirt, i gcorp 's i gcnámh é,
Ca bhfuil a locht i gcois ná i láimh dhe?
Ní seirgtheach fann ná seandach feosach,
Leibide cam ná gandal geoiseach,
Meall gan chuma ná sumach gan síneadh é,
Ach lansa cumasach buinneamhach bríomhar!
Ní deacair a mheas nach spreas gan bhrí
Bhí ceangailte ar nasc ar teasc ag mnaoi,   620
Gan chnámh gan chumas gan chuma gan chom
Gan ghrá gan chumann gan fuinneamh gan fonn,
Do scaipfeadh i mbroinn aon mhaighre mná
Le catachas dradhain an groidhire breá,
Mar chuireann sé i bhfeidhm gan mhoill gan bhréig
Le cumas a bhaill is le loigheamh a ghéag
Gur crobhaire crothadh go cothrom gan cháim é
Le fonn na fola is le fothram na sláinte.

Leis sin ná hiarrsa, a Riain réaltach,
Meilleadh myriad le riail gan éifeacht,   630
Scaoil a chodladh gan chochall gan chuíbhreach

180

With their prattle and noise while drink is pouring,
Since the essence which God's Son gave so freely
Matured without priest or marriage decree?
Widely found, strong, plentiful, brave,
In large supply is this free generation.
'Tis often I see them vigorous, blooming,
Powerful, hearty and in good shape,
No flaw do I see, neither squinting nor blindness
In any woman's nurtured by-child;
They're stronger and quicker and firmer and larger
In form and ability than the offspring of marriage!

h) *The Living Proof (607-628)*

And now 'tis easy to prove what I say,
With one of them here among us today.
Do you see him yonder so gentle and quiet?
Bring him over here to the table.
Look at him closely, though he is young,
He's well set up and firm and strong,
He's a rouser in size, in body and bone,
Where is the fault in his foot or his hand?
He's not withered and weak, or fleshless and old,
A twisted fool or a pot-bellied gander,
A shapeless lump or a lad without growth,
But a powerful, vigorous, robust youth!
'Tis easy to see 'twas no spineless thing
Tied to a woman's apron string,
Without bone or strength or shape or girth,
Without love or affection or force or will
Who would strew in the womb of a beautiful lady
In the white heat of passion so fine a baby.
For he plainly shows and none can deny
By the power of his limbs and the way they lie
The strong lad was conceived at a perfect level
In desire of the blood and in lusty health.

i) *He Appeals for Sexual Freedom (629-644)*

So, Queen of the stars, then, seek not to ruin
Thousands and thousands with a pointless rule.
Let the seed of the churl and the noble strain

181

Síol an bhodaigh 's an mhogalfhuil mhaíteach,
Scaoil fá chéile de réir nádúra
An síolbhach séad is an braon lábúrtha.
Fógair féilteach tré gach tíortha
D'óg is d'aosta saorthoil síolraigh.
Cuirfidh an dlí seo gaois i nGaelaibh
Is tiocfaidh ann brí mar bhí 'na laochaibh,
Ceapfaidh sé com is drom is dóirne
Ag fearaibh an domhain mar Gholl mac Mórna,   640
Gealfaidh an spéir, beidh éisc i líonta,
Talamh an tslé' go léir fá luíonna,
Fir agus mná go brách dá bhíthin
Ag sinm do cháil le gárdas aoibhnis'.

III

Tréis bheith tamall don ainnir ag éisteacht,
Léim 'na seasamh go tapaidh gan fhoighne,
Labhair sí leis agus loise 'na súile
Is rabhartaí feirge feille aici fúthu:

'Dar coróin na Craige, marach le géilleadh
Dod chló, dod ainnise, is d'easnamh do chéille,   650
Is d'am na huirrime 'on chuideachta shéimh seo,
An ceann lem ingin do sciobfainn ded chaolscrog,
Do leagfainn anuas de thuairt fán mbórd thú,
Is b'fhada le lua gach cuairt dá ngeobhainn ort,
Stróicfinn sreanga do bheatha le fonn ceart,
Is sheolfainn t'anam go hAcheron tonntach!

Ní fiú liom freagra freastail a thabhairt ort,
A shnamhaire galair nach aiteas do labhartha!
Ach 'neosad feasta do mhaithe na cúirte
An nós 'nar cailleadh an ainnir nárbh fhiú thú.   660
Do bhí sí lag, gan ba gan púntaibh,
Bhí sí i bhfad gan teas gan clúdadh,
Cortha dá saol, ar strae á seoladh
Ó phosta go p'léar gan ghaol gan chóngas,

Lie together without condom or hindrance.
Let the offspring of affluence and the plebeian stock
Mingle as nature may fashion their lot.
Proclaim at intervals in every region
The right of all to unshackled breeding.
This law will make the Gael sagacious
And restore the ancient warrior force.
It will make men again like Goll MacMórna[11]
With waist and back and the fists of Trojans.
The sky will clear, the fish abound,
The moorland teem with herbs all round,
For that men and women will ever after
Be singing your praises 'mid happy laughter.'

Part III. The Girl Replies

a) *She Threatens Violence (645-656)*

When the girl had been listening for a while
She jumped to her feet quickly, impatiently,
She spoke to him with flashing eyes
And tides of perilous wrath behind them:

'By the crown of Crag, were I not well aware
Of your wretched condition, lack of sense and shape,
And of the time of respect for this noble house,
With my nails your goose-neck from your head I'd tear.
I'd knock you down there by the table
And the blows I'd strike would take long to relate.
The threads of your life I'd slit with a will
And send your soul to the nether river![12]

b) *The Old Man's Young Bride (657-678)*

I think you're not worth a considered reply,
You diseased old wretch, your words are absurd!
But I'll tell the worthies of the court
How the young woman died who was far too good for you.
She had no means, neither cattle nor gold,
She was for long without heat, without clothes,
Weary of life, on the road all the day,
From pillar to post, without friend or relation,

Gan scíth gan spás de lá ná d'oíche
Ag stríocadh an aráin ó mhná nár chuí léi.
Do gheall an fear so dreas sócúil di,
Gheall an spreas di teas is clúdadh,
Cothrom glan is ba le crú dhi
Is codladh fada ar leabain chlúimh dhi,   670
Teallaí teo is móin a daoithin,
Ballaí fód gan leoithne gaoithe,
Fothain is díon ón síon 's ón spéir dhi
Is olann is líon le sníomh chun éadaigh.
Dob fheasach don tsaol 's don phéist seo láithreach
Nach taithneamh ná téamh ná aonphioc grá dho
Cheangail an péarla maorga mná so
Ach easnamh go léir – ba déirc léi an tsástacht!

Ba dubhach an fuadar suairceas oíche:
Smúid is ualach, duais is líonadh,   680
Lúithní lua' is guaillí caola
Is glúine crua chomh fuar le hoighre,
Cosa feoite dóite ón ngríosaigh
Is colainn bhreoite dhreoite chríonna!
An bhfuil stuaire beo ná feofadh liath
Ag cuail dá short bheith pósta riamh,
Nár chuardaigh fós fá dhó le bliain
Cé buachaill óg í, feoil, nó iasc?
'S an feoiteach fuar so suas léi sínte
Dreoite duairc, gan bhua gan bhíogadh.   690
Ó! Cár mhuar di bualadh bríomhar
Ar nós an diabhail dhá uair gach oíche!

Ní dóch go dtuigir gurb ise ba chiontach,
Ná fós go gclisfeadh ar laige le tamhandacht
An maighre mascalach carthannach ciúintais
– Is deimhin go bhfaca sí a mhalairt de mhúineadh!
Ní labharfadh focal dá mb'obair an oíche
Is thabharfadh cothrom do stollaire bríomhar,
Go brách ar siúl nár dhiúltaigh riamh é
Ar chnámh a cúil 's a súile iata.   700

Without rest or respite by day or night
Getting her bread from women she despised.
This man promised her a pleasant life,
The good-for-nothing vowed her heat and clothing,
Proper treatment and cows to milk,
Long hours of sleep in a bed of down,
Heated hearths and plenty of peat,
Stone walls shielding her from the breeze,
Shelter from tempest and from sky,
Wool and flax to spin for ply.
This reptile knew – and the world, besides –
No liking or warming or crumb of love
Had joined this splendid pearl of a wife to him
But solid want – charity to her was to get enough!

c) *The Old Man's Impotence (679-692)*

Entertainment at night was no cheery prospect
– But gloom and a burden of heartfelt distress,
Leaden legs and narrow shoulders,
Two rocky knees like ice-capped boulders,
Shrivelled feet in the ashes roasted,
A body withered and feeble and mouldering!
Is the girl alive who would not go grey
To be wed to the skeleton even for a day,
Who in the space of a year never twice tried
Whether she were boy or flesh or pike?
And the frozen stump beside her lying
Decayed, morose, inert and useless,
While she would need a vigorous threshing
Twice a night in the heat of passion!

d) *How She Would Stimulate Him (693-720)*

You will hardly consider that she was to blame,
Or that feeble inertness would cause her to fail;
The strapping beauty, kind, quiet and gentle
Certainly had quite a different training!
Not a word would she say if at night she must labour,
A vigorous man she would treat with fairness;
She never refused the on-going play
On the broad of her back with her two eyes veiled.

185

Ní thabharfadh preab le stailc mhíchuíosach,
Fogha mar chat ná sraic ná scríob air,
Ach í go léir 'na slaod comh-sínte,
Taobh ar thaobh 's a géag 'na thimpeall,
Ó scéal go scéal ag bréagadh a smaointe,
Béal ar bhéal 's ag méaraíocht síos air.
Is minic do chuir sí a cos taobh 'nonn de
Is chuimil a brush ó chrios go glún de,
Sciobadh an phluid 's an chuilt dá ghúnga
Ag spriongar 's ag sult le moirt gan súchas.   710
Níor chabhair dhi cigilt ná cuimilt ná fáscadh,
Fogha dá huillinn, dá hingin ná a sála,
Is nár dom aithris mar chaitheadh sí an oíche
Ag fáscadh an chnaiste 's ag searradh 's ag síneadh,
Ag feacadh na ngéag 's an t-éadach fúithi,
A ballaibh go léir 's a déid ar lúthchrith,
Go loinnir an lae gan néall do dhúbhadh uirthi,
Ag imirt ó thaobh go taobh 's ag ionfairt
– Nach furas don lobhar so labhairt ar mhná
Is gan fuinneamh 'na chom ná cabhair 'na chnámha!   720

Má d'imigh an mhodhamhail bhí trom 'na ghá
'S gur deineadh an fhoghail seo, gabhaimse a páirt;
An bhfuil sionnach ar sliabh, ná iasc i dtrá,
Ná fiolar le fiach, ná fia le fán
Chomh fada gan chiall le bliain ná lá
A chaitheamh gan bia 's a bhfiach le fáil?
An aithnid díbh féin sa tsaol so cá'il
An t-ainmhí claon ná an féithid fáin
A phiocfadh an chré, ná an fraoch, ná an fál,
Is fiorthann go slaodach is féar le fáil?   730
Aithris gan mhoill, a chladhaire chráite,
Freagair mé, faghaimse feidhm id ráite!
Cá bhfuil do dhíth ag suí chun béile
Ar caitheadh le mí aici i dtíos na féile?
An laigide an chúil nó an lúide an láthair
Fiche milliún má shiúil le ráithe ann?
Mairg id cheann, a sheandaigh thamhanda,
An eagal leat ganntan am do dhúla?
An dóch, a ghliogaire buile, gur baol leat

She would not bounce in a stubborn sulk,
Claw like a cat or tug or scrape him,
But lie down quietly, complaisant,
Side by side with her arm around him,
Coaxing his thoughts from point to point,
Her mouth on his mouth while she plied her fingers.
She'd often throw her leg astride him
And rub her brush from his thigh to his knee;
She'd snatch the blanket and quilt from his loins,
Trifling and playing with the cheerless old blighter.
Neither tickling, rubbing nor squeezing availed,
The spur of her elbow, heel or nail;
It shames me to tell how she'd pass the night,
Squeezing the fossil, shrugging and stretching,
Twisting her limbs with her clothes beneath her,
Her members and teeth all in a tremble,
To the crack of dawn without a wink of sleep,
Moving and stirring from side to side;
– How easily the weakling can talk about women,
With no power in his body or bone or sinew!

e) *Justifying Her Adultery (721-748)*

If the lady went off in her crying need
And the trespass was done, I take her part here:
Is there a fox on the moor or a fish on the shore,
Or a prowling eagle, or a stag on the slope
Such a fool as to wait for a year or a day
When the food can be got at right away?
Do you yourselves know where in the world
Is the beast of prey or the wandering bird
That would browse the clay or the dike or the heath
With wheat-grass and meadow-grass profuse on the lea?
Speak up now, at once, you wretched scoundrel,
Let me see reason in your answer!
What have you lost when you sit to your meal
If her household dispense for the month has been liberal?
Is the corner the worse, or the place the less
If twenty millions this season traversed it?
Bad cess to you for a stubborn old fool,
Is it scarcity you dread in your time of desire?
You crazy prater, do you then fear

Ól na Sionainne t'rim ná a taoscadh,   740
Trá na farraige is tarraingt an tsáile
Is clár na mara a scaipeadh le scála?
Breathain in am ar leamhas do smaointe
Is ceangail do cheann le banda timpeall!
Seachain i dtráth, ná fág do chiall
Le heagla mná bheith fáilteach fial;
Dá gcaitheadh sí an lá le cách á riar,
Beidh tuilleadh is do shá-se ar fáil 'na ndiaidh...

Is mithid dom chroí bheith líonta 'e léithe
Is m'iongantas tríd gach smaointe baotha:
Cad do bheir scaoilte ó chuíbhreach céile
In eaglais sínsir suím na cléire?   760
Mo chrá gan leigheas, mo threighid dom fháscadh,
Is láidir m'fhoighne is laghad mo ráige
Is méad a mbíom ar díth gan éinne
Is mian ár gcroí fá shnaídhm na héide!
Is bocht an radharc do mhaighdin ghámhar
Toirt is taibhse a mboill, 's a mbreáthacht,
Bloscadh a n-aghaidh is soilse a ngáire,
Coirp is coim is toill ar táimhchrith,
Úireacht, áilleacht, bláth is óige,
Ramhdas cnámh is meáchan feola,   770
Martas trom is drom gan suathadh,
Neart, gan dabht, is fonn gan fuaradh.
Bíonn sealbh gach só acu ar bhórd na saoithe,
Earra agus ór chun óil is aoibhnis,
Clúmh chun loighe acu is soill chun bídh acu,
Plúr is milseacht, meidhir is fíonta.
Is gnáthach cumasach iomadach óg iad
Is tá's againne gur fuil is gur feoil iad.

Cumha ní ghlacfainn le cafairí coillte,
Snamhairí galair ná searraigh gan soilse,   780

188

You'll drink up or drain the Shannon with your cup?
That the sea will ebb and its current recede
And its level top be dispersed with a bowl?
Examine your foolish thoughts in time
And bind your head round with the cuckold's band!
Take heed in good time, don't take leave of your senses
For fear that a woman is welcoming, generous,
If she gave it to everyone throughout the day,
You'd have more than enough when she came your way...

*This section is brought to a close in eight verses which sharply contrast the
young, virile man with the decrepit and impotent old one. Then she moves to
a new topic:*

f) *Clerical Celibacy (757-778)*

It's time my heart was filled with greyness
In wonderment at ideas so crazy:
Why are the clerics of the older Church
– All of them – free of the marriage yoke?
My incurable torment, my oppressing pain,
Strong is my patience and restraint,
Considering how many of us have no man near
And the man of our choice in the dress of a priest!
For a needy virgin 'tis a very sad sight
The size and splendour of their limbs, they're so fine.
Their radiance of face, the light of their smile,
Body, waist and thighs torpidly trembling.
Freshness, beauty, bloom and youth
Depth of bone and weight of flesh,
A solid torso, a steady back,
Strength, indeed; desire uncooled.
Theirs is ease at cultured tables,
Goods and gold for drink and entertainment,
Beds of down and pork to eat,
Flour and dainties, wines and glee,
They're usually powerful, numerous, young,
And we have no doubt that they're flesh and blood.

g) *Kinds of Priest (779-806)*

I would not mind the gelded praters,
Ailing cringers or ignorant striplings,

189

Ach márlaigh bhodacha, tollairí tréana
I dtámhaíl chodlata is obair gan déanamh...!
Creidim gan bhréig gur mhéin le roinnt díobh
Feilleadh le féile – daor ní bheinnse,
Cothrom, ní cóir an t-ord le chéile
Chrochadh le corda, ghóil is dhaoradh;
Bás na droinge go deimhin ní ghráfainn,
Lán na loinge chun duine ní bháfainn!
Cuid acu bíodh gur rícigh riamh iad,
Is cuid acu bhíos gan ríomh gan riail leo,   790
Cinntigh chrua gan trua gan tréithe,
Fíochmhar fuar, is fuath do bhéithe –
Tuille acu tá níos fearr ná a chéile,
Tuilte le grá is le grásta féile;
Is minic a buaitear buaibh is gréithe,
Cuigeann is cruach de chuairt na cléire,
Is minic lem chuimhne maíodh a dtréithe
Is iomad a ngníomhartha fíorghlic féithe,
Is minic do chuala ar fuaid na tíre
Siosarnach luath á lua go líonmhar,   800
Is chonaic mé taibhseach roinnt dá ramsa
Is uimhir dá gclainn ar shloinnte falsa.
Baineann sé fáscadh as lár mo chléibhse
A gcaitear dá sláinte ar mhná treasaosta,
Is turraing sa tír chun díth na mbéithe
Ar cuireadh gan bhrí den tsíolrach naofa.

Is dealbh an diachair dhianghoirt d'Éire
– Ar chailleamair riamh le riail gan éifeacht.
Fágaim fútsa, a chnú na céille,
Fáth na cúise is cumha na cléire,   810
Is meallta millte loighid, dom dhóighse,
Is dall gan radharc mé, soilsigh m'eolas!
Aithris, ós cuimhin leat caínt na bhfáige
Is aspail an Rí ba bíogach ráite:
Ca bhfuil na comhachta d'orda' an dúladh
Is calcadh na feola i gcró na cumha so?
Pól, dar liom, ní dúirt le héinne
An pósadh dhiúltadh, ach drúis a shéanadh,
Scaradh led ghaol dá mhéid de ghnaoi

But lusty lads and robust youths
Lying drugged in sleep with work still to do...!
I believe indeed that some would like
To revert to pleasure – I would not be severe!
In fairness, the order as a whole
Should not be seized, condemned and hanged with a cord;
The death of all I'd by no means care for,
Because of one I'd not drown the whole ship's crew!
Although some of them have always been wastrels,
And some of them are hard to make out,
Misers and harsh, without pity or parts,
Fierce and cold, hating women;
Some of them, again, are better than others,
Abounding in love and in liberal graces.
– Cattle and goods, butter and turf
Are often gained in the wake of the clergy.
'Tis often I remember their qualities mentioned,
And their many guileful, lecherous deeds;
'Tis often I heard the lively murmur
Of whispers rustling through the country;
'Tis plainly I saw a share of their romping
And many of their offspring with spurious names.
It gives me a pang in my breast to see
Their health expended on middle-aged women,
While the country's in haste to destroy the girls,
Who were idly deprived of the sacred seed.

h) *She Argues Against Clerical Celibacy (807-828)*

For Ireland it's been a most grievous affliction
– All we have lost by a pointless rule:
To you I leave it, O Gem of Discretion:
The cause of the matter, the yearning of clerics.[13]
I think they're deluded, in sorry plight,
Dark is my vision, enlighten me, tell,
Since you remember what prophets have told
And the King's apostles whose words had such force,
Where are the powers that ordained desire
And the hardening of flesh in sorrow and gyves?
Paul, I think, never said anyone must
Abstain from marriage – but only from lust:
Turn from your kinsman, though never so dear,

Agus ceangal led shaol, is claobh, led mhnaoi.
Is obair gan bhrí do mhnaoi mar táimse
Focail an dlí seo shuíomh dod láthair,
Is cuimhin leat féin, a phéarla, an Taibhse,
Suíomh gach scéil is léir duit soilseach,
Binnghuth buan is bua na mbréithre
Is caínt an Uain ná luafar bréagach,
Dia nárbh áil leis Máthair aonta,
Is riail gach fáidhe i bhfábhar béithe...

Scalladh mo chléibh! Is baoth mo smaointe
Ag tagairt ar chéile i gcaorthaibh tínte;
Is deacair dom súil le súchas d'fháil
'S gan fear in aghaidh triúir sa Mhumhain dá mná!
Ó thárla an ceantar gann so gámhar,
Fáintibh go fann 's an t-am so práinneach,
Fódla folamh is fothram ag fiaile,
Is óga an phobail ag cromadh 's ag liathadh,   850
Aonta fada go dealbh ná foidhnigh
D'éinne ar thalamh – is fear éigin faghaimse!
Ceangail i dtráth go tláth fán úim iad
Is as sin go brách ach fágtar fúinn iad!'

33. The Old Man

The motif of the old man married to a young girl is widely exploited in world literature; it is central to Brian Merriman's Midnight Court *(No. 43). In keeping with the comic and absurd facets of such a marriage, the subject is dealt with in a rollicking, rakish manner in this lively song.*

The three that did get me to wed the old neddy,
Mother, father and prieshteen, all of them eager,
Home they went afterwards, home to their feasting,
Now my friends and companions scarce ever come near me.

> *No, no, you old fogey, with you I'll not go,*
> *No, no, you old fogey, with you I'll not go,*
> *No, no, you old fogey, with you I'll not go,*
> *'Tis a fret that old age will cleave to youth so!*

'Twas advice that I got, out walking the road
From a rogue of a prieshteen to marry the old one;
'Twas little he cared but to pocket the gold,
If I spent my future depending on neighbours next door.

I married the old man, I must have been crazy,
That much I did on advice of relations;
Off to his home then, alas for the tale!
I got up in the morning and wished death would take me.

If I found my old man drowned in a boghole,
I'd have him brought home and prepared for the wake,
I'd padlock the door and pocket the key
And walk out in the young lads' company.

If I was possessed of a horse and a bridle,
An iron bit and a saddle to ride him,
I'd bring my old man out to the highland
And bring home in the saddle my strapping young viking.

I went up to Cork for provisions to wake him,
Tobacco and snuff, for his coffin the makings,
I landed back sorrowful, exhausted and ailing
To find my old man roasting potatoes!

34. Iníon An Phailitínigh

Ó! lá breá aoibhinn maragaidh
   's mé a' gabháil thrí Bhail' Ó Síoda,
Cé casfaí ins a' tslí orm ach
   iníon a' Phailitínigh?
Ó! d' fhiosaruigh sí fios m'ainime,
   'nó goidé an baile ó go mbíonn tú?
A' dtiocfá féin abhaile liom
   seal i dtigh mo mhuinntre?'
'Sé dubhart, 'Is buachaill greanta mé
   do chomhnuíonn i gCoirínibh.'

'Má thréigeann tú an t-aifreann
   do gheó tú mé le pósa,
Mar a dhein mo cháirde féinig is
   a maireann eile beo aca.
Gheó tú ór is airgead
   is talamh gan aon chíos liom,
Agus litir ó *Mhister Oliver*
   go bhfuil m'athair caithte, críonna,
Is cailín deas chun taistil leat,
   más meón leat Pailitíneach.'

Do dhruideas-sa 'n-a h-aice siúd
   is do thugas dí cúpla póigín:
'Is má théim-se féin abhaile leat
   an bhfagha mé tú le pósa?'

34. The Palatine's Daughter

By a government policy decision, Palatine families rendered homeless in the wars with France were brought to Dublin in 1709. Of these, 157 were sent to the country, particularly to Limerick and Kerry, where they made very progressive farmers. Of the Adare Palatines Arthur Young writes:

> *They are remarkable for the goodness and cleanliness of their houses. The women are very industrious, reap the corn, plough the ground sometimes, and do whatever work may be going on; they also spin, and make their children do the same.*

Hence the young man figured in our song might well consider himself fortunate. The place names Ballyseedy and Currans in the Tralee–Castleisland region show that it is a Kerry song. A Palatine colony was settled here about 1745. Some twenty years later a Mr Oliver of Castle Oliver in Rathkeale planted a colony of Palatines there, and the Mr Oliver of our song may well be connected with that family.

O! One fine market day
   As I was passing through Ballyseedy,
Who should I meet on my way
   But the daughter of the Palatine.
O! she asked me my name
   'And what village do you hail from?
Would you come back home with me
   To my parents' house a while?'
I said 'I am a tidy lad
   And I hail from the Curreenies.'

'If the Mass you will give over,
   You will get myself to wed,
Just as all my own friends have done
   And those that live with them as well.
You'll get silver and gold
   And land free from rent with me,
And a letter from *Mister Oliver*
   That my dad's worn out and old,
And a pretty girl to go with you,
   If you fancy a Palatine.'

I moved up beside her
   And I kissed her a few times.
'And if I come home with you
   Will I get yourself to wed?'

'Sé dubhairt sí, 'Ná bíodh eagal ort,
   tair liom is míle fáilte,
Is gheó tú le toil m'athar mé,
   's gan dearmad mo mháithrín,
Gheó tú stoc ar thalamh liom
   is mairfimíd go sásta.'

Is anois tá mo dhuainín críochnuithe
   's gan peann ná duhh im dhearnain,
Do thug sí an t-óigfhear barrfhionn lé
   abhaile go dtí n-a máthair.
Do chríochnuíodar an maraga
   is bhí sé annsan 'n-a mháistir,
Fuair sé tigh is talamh lé
   'gus iothala chluthmhar shásta,
Is annsan do dhein sé Caitliceach
   den ainnir mhilis mhánla.

35. Snaidhm an Ghrá

Ise: 'Is mo ghrá go léir tu, agus Dé do bheatha chúm!
        Mo ghrá do shúile, agus t'éadan leathan geal,
        Mo ghrá do chroí, nár smaoing ar mh'atharrach,
        Mo ghrá mh'fhear óg, 's is é mo bhrón bheith sgartha
            leat!'

Eisean: 'Níl id ghrá-sa ach mar a bheadh mám 'en tsneachta
          'muigh,
        Nú cúr lae Márta, 'chaithfeadh caise dhe,
        Nú puis den ghaoith thig do dhruím na fairrge,
        Nú tuile shléi bheadh t'réis lae fearthanna!'

132

She said, 'Don't be a bit afraid,
  A thousand welcomes! Come!
My father will be willing
  And my mother too for sure.
You'll get livestock on land with me
  And we'll live happy and secure.'

Now, my little poem is over
  And my pen and ink are laid aside,
For she brought her fair-haired young man
  With her home to her mother.
They made the bargain then
  And he became the master;
He got house and land with her
  And a haggard warm and tidy;
– And then he made a Catholic
  Of his gentle, graceful bride.

35. The Love Knot

*A Kerry version of this Cork song provides it with a context and background
typical for Gaelic songs of its type: the girl's lover, being poor, was disregarded
by her parents, who married her to a rich man. On the morning of the wedding,
word was brought to her that her lover lay critically ill. So she went to visit
him and found him very weak, whereupon the poetic dialogue took place as given
below. He died while she was saying the last verse and she lay down by his side
and died also. Although they were buried at some distance from each other, a
tree grew up out of each grave and bent towards each other until ultimately
finger-like antennae from each interlocked. Hence the title* Snaidhm an Ghrá
– The Love Knot, *with a symbolisation found also in British balladry.*

Girl: 'I love you only; you are welcome to me;
  I love your eyes, your face broad and bright,
  Your heart, that has not thought another love to find,
  My darling young man, alas, to be no more with you!'

Man: 'Your love is nought but snow that melts in the hand,
  Or spray in March, cast by the brook on land,
  Or a breath of wind along the surface of the sea,
  Or a mountain torrent following on one day's rain.'

Ise: "S cá bhfeacaís mo ghrá-sa ná mo pháirt let atharrach?
Ná dul ag ól leó ar bhórd go ceanasach?
Mar nár smaoingeas im chroí ná im aigne
Luí 'n-a gclúid, agus gan tú bheith ceangailthe.'

Eisean: "S go deimhin, a mhianaigh, níor smaoingeas masla
dhuit,
Ná tú bhreith liúm gan cead ód bhantharlain,
'Dtaobh gan amhras gur bh'fhearr liom agam tu
Ná'n dá asbal déag, is ná maor an anama.'

Ise: 'Glaéidh ar Dhia go dian chun t'anama,
'S ar a' Maighdean Naomhtha, 'sí céile is fearra dhuit,
'Sí thúrfaidh saor tú lá dhaortha an anama;
Séan mo ghrá-sa 'gus mo pháirt 'n fhaid a mhairfe tú!'

Eisean: 'Ní shéanfad do ghrá-sa ná do pháirt 'n fhaid a mhairfe
mé,
Ná go ceann seacht mbliain t'réis dul 'on talamh dom;
Mar níor shín do chéile riamh fós ar leabaidh leat,
'S go deimhin, nuair a shínfidh, sínfead-sa eadaraibh!'

Ise: "S nách gránda an fuath é, t'réis muarán ceanais duit,
Cuir mh'fhir phósda go deó deó i n-earraid liom,
A' troid 's a' coimheascar, a' bruíon 's ag acharann,
'S gan tusa beó 'gam chun mo sgéal duit 'aithris!'

36. Caoineadh na dTrí Muire

A Pheadair, a Aspail, a' bhfaca tú mo ghrá bán?
Och, ochón is ochón ó!
Chonaic me ar ball é dá chéasadh ag an ngarda.
Och, ochón is ochón ó!

Girl: 'And where did you see me love or favour another?
Or go drinking with them boldly at the tavern board?
For I never thought to lie in their embrace
Even when you were not yet bound to me.'

Man: 'And indeed, my dear one, I meant no offence to you,
Nor to bring you with me till your foster mother did
approve,
Although in truth I would rather you
Than the twelve apostles, or the guardian of my soul.'

Girl: 'Pray fervently to God that He your soul may save,
And to the Holy Virgin, who best your peace can make,
She will deliver you on the day of doom,
And while you live, reject my love and friendship!'

Man: 'While I live your love and friendship I'll not reject,
Nor for seven years further in the grave,
Your wedded mate with you abed has not yet lain,
And when he does, be sure I'll lie between the two of you!'

Girl: 'My deep love you now requite with horrid hate,
Setting my husband at strife forever with his own mate,
Fighting, struggling, quarrelling and disputing,
With you yourself no longer living to tell my story to!'

36. Lament of the Three Marys

'A keen *with this name used to be chanted at funerals and wakes in Glendun, County Antrim. Three women took part in it and keened it, as they marched in the procession to the grave. Mrs Nellie O'Neill, who died in Glendun some years ago, had acted in this way as one of the three Marys.'*[1]

I print the Lament in the Connemara version sung by Seosamh Ó hÉanaí, which differs in some respects from the usual one. Characteristic are the 'seal-skin suit' of stanza 5 and the impromptu style of stanza 4.

Apostle Peter, did you see my bright love?
Woe, alas, and woe is me!
I saw him being crucified by the guard a while since,
Woe, alas, and woe is me!

Maise, cén fear breá sin ar chrann na páise?
Och, ochón, is ochón ó!
An é nach n-aithníonn tú do mhac, a mháithrín?
Och, ochón is ochón ó!

An é sin an maicín a d'iompair mé trí ráithe?
Och, ochón is ochón ó!
Nó an é sin an maicín a rugadh ins an stábla?
Och, ochón is ochón ó!

Nó an é sin an maicín a hoileadh in ucht Mháire?
Och, ochón is ochón ó!
A mhicín mhuirneach tá do bhéal 's do shróinín gearrtha.
Och, ochón is ochón ó!

Is cuireadh culaith róin air le spídiúlacht óna námhaid.
Och, ochón is ochón ó!
Is cuireadh coróin spíonta ar a mhullach álainn.
Och, ochón is ochón ó!

Is crochadh suas é ar ghuaillí arda.
Och, ochón is ochón ó!
Is buaileadh 'nuas é faoi leacrachaí na sráide.
Och, ochón is ochón ó!

Is cuireadh go Cnoc Calvaraí é ag méadú ar a pháise.
Och, ochón is ochón ó!
Bhí sé 'g iompar na croich' agus Síomóin lena shála.
Och, ochón is ochón ó!

Maise, buailigí mé fhéin ach ná bainí le mo mháithrín.
Och, ochón is ochón ó!
Maróimid thú fhéin agus buailfimid do mháithrín.
Och, ochón is ochón ó!

Is cuireadh tairní maola tríotha a chosa 'gus a lámha.
Och, ochón is ochón ó!
Is cuireadh an tsleá thrína bhrollach álainn.
Och, ochón is ochón ó!

Maise, éist a mháthair is ná bí cráite!
Och, ochón is ochón ó!

O, who's that fine man on the cross of passion?
Woe, alas, and woe is me!
O, mother, don't you know your own son?
Woe, alas, and woe is me!

Is that the son I bore for nine months?
Woe, alas, and woe is me!
And is that the son was born in the manger?
Woe, alas, and woe is me!

And is that the son reared in the lap of Mary?
Woe, alas, and woe is me!
Dear son, your mouth and nose are gashed and bleeding.
Woe, alas, and woe is me!

Through spite they dressed him in a suit of sealskin.
Woe, alas, and woe is me!
On his lovely head they put a crown of thorns.
Woe, alas, and woe is me!

He was hoisted up on shoulders high,
Woe, alas, and woe is me!
He was thrown down on pavements of stone.
Woe, alas, and woe is me!

To Calvary Hill he was sent, his torment to increase.
Woe, alas, and woe is me!
He bore his cross with Simon at his heels.
Woe, alas, and woe is me!

Strike myself, but my mother leave in peace.
Woe, alas, and woe is me!
We'll kill yourself and give her a beating.
Woe, alas, and woe is me!

Blunt nails they hammered through hands and feet then.
Woe, alas, and woe is me!
And through his lovely breast the spear went.
Woe, alas, and woe is me!

Mother, hush now, and stop your grieving.
Woe, alas, and woe is me!

Tá mná mo chaointe le breith fós, a mháithrín.
Och, ochón is ochón ó!

37. Mo Bhrón ar an bhFarraige

Mo bhrón ar an bhfarraige,
Is í atá mór,
's í ag gabháil idir mé,
Is mo mhíle stór.

Fágadh sa mbaile mé
Ag déanamh bróin,
Gan aon tsúil thar sáile liom,
Choíche ná go deo.

Mo léan nach bhfuil mise
'Gus mo mhuirnín bán
I gCúige Laighean
Nó i gContae an Chláir!

Mo bhrón nach bhfuil mise
'Gus mo mhíle grá
Ar bord loinge
Ag triall ar Mheiriocá!

Leaba luachra
A bhí fúm aréir,
Is chaith mé amach é
Le teas an lae.

Tháinig mo ghrá-sa
Le mo thaobh,
Guala ar ghualainn
Agus béal ar bhéal.

Women unborn yet will do my keening.
Woe, alas, and woe is me!

1. Róis Ní Ógáin, *Duanaire Gaedhilge* I, Dublin 1921, p. 115.

37. My Grief on the Sea

Douglas Hyde tells us that he recorded this little gem of a love poem from an old woman who was living in the middle of a bog in County Roscommon.

My grief on the sea,
How massively it rolls!
For it comes between me
And the love of my soul.

I was left at home
A prey to woe and pain,
With no eye watching oversea
For me ever to set sail.

My grief and affliction!
Would my love and I were
In the province of Leinster,
Or the county of Clare!

O were I and my darling
Together once more
On a ship in full sail
To America's shore!

On a bed of green rushes
Last night I lay,
And I cast it outside
With the heat of the day;

And my own love
Came to my side,
His shoulder to my shoulder,
And his lips to mine.

38. Droimeann Donn Dílis

A Dhroimeann donn dílis,
A shíoda na mbó,
Cá ngabhann tú san oíche
'S cá mbíonn tú sa ló?
Bíonn mise ar na coillte
Is mo bhuachaill im' chomhair,
Agus d'fhág sé siúd mise
Ag sileadh na ndeor.

Níl fearann, níl tíos agam,
Níl fíonta ná ceol,
Níl flaithe im' choimhdeacht,
Níl saoithe ná sló,
Acht ag síoról an uisce
Go minic sa ló,
Agus beathuisce is fíon
Ag mo náimhde ar bord.

Dá bhfaighinn-se cead aighnis
Nó radharc ar an gcoróin,
Sasanaigh do leidhbfinn
Mar do leidhbfinn seanbhróg,
Trí chnocaibh, trí ailltibh
'S trí ghleanntaibh dubha ceoigh,
Agus siúd mar a bhréagfainn-se
An Droimeann donn óg.

38. Dear Brown Drimmin

Droimeann was formerly written Druim-fhionn *'white-backed'; here it stands for 'the white-backed cow'. A comparison between different versions shows that this rather cryptic song is political and Jacobite. The king referred to in stanza 3 is King James, and* Droimeann *stands for Ireland.*

> *O dear brown Drimmin,*
> *Silk of the kine,*
> *Where do you go at night,*
> *And where are you in day-time?*
> I am in the woods
> With my herd by my side,
> And now he has left me
> Weeping out my eyes.
>
> Neither land nor house have I,
> Music nor wines,
> Princes for company,
> The common nor the wise,
> But water for my drink
> Often through the day,
> On my enemies' table
> Whiskey and wine.
>
> If I got the right to plead,
> Or could see the Throne,
> The English I would trounce
> As I would trounce an old brogue,
> Through hills, through heights
> And through dark dewy glens,
> And so would I entice
> Brown young Drimmin.

39. An Chúileann

An bhfaca tú an chúileann, 's í ag siúl ar na bóithre,
Maidin gheal drúchta 's gan smúit ar a bróga?
Is iomaí ógánach súilghlas ag tnúth lena pósadh,
Acht ní fhaigheann siad mo rún-sa ar an gcuntas is dóigh leo.

An bhfaca tú mo bhábán lá breá 's í 'na haonar,
A cúl dualach drisleanach go slinneán síos léithi?
Mil ar an óigbhean 's rós breá 'na héadan,
'S is dóigh le gach spreasán gur leannán leis féin í.

An bhfaca tú mo spéirbhean 's í taobh leis an toinn,
Fáinní óir ar a méaraibh 's í ag réiteach a cinn?
Is é dúirt an Paorach 'bhí ina mhaor ar an loing,
Go mb'fhearr leis aige féin í ná Éire gan roinn.

40. Ceann Dubh Dílis

A chinn duibh dhílis dhílis dhílis,
    cuir do lámh mhín gheal tharm anall;
a bhéilín meala a bhfuil baladh na tíme air,
    's duine gan chroí nach dtiúrfadh dhuit grá!

Tá cailíní ar an mbaile seo ar buile is ar buaireamh,
    ag tarraingt a ngruaige is á ligean le gaoith,
ar mo shonsa an scafaire is fearr ins na tuatha,
    ach thréigfinn an méid sin ar rún dil mo chroí.

'S a chinn duibh dhílis dhílis dhílis,
    cuir do lámh mhín gheal tharm anall;
a bhéilín meala a bhfuil baladh na tíme air,
    's duine gan chroí nach dtiúrfadh dhuit grá!

39. The Coolin

Coolin stands for cúil-fhionn *'a head of fair hair', also for the possessor of such a head: 'the fair-haired one'. The treatment of the lady in this poem, like that of Drimmin in No. 38, is veiled and the last line suggests that here too the intent is political.*

Have you seen the fair-haired one walking on the roads,
With no dust upon her shoes in the bright dews of the morn?
There's many a grey-eyed youth that desires her for his own,
But they will not win my love in the way that they may hope.

And have you seen my dear on a fine day and she alone,
In sparkling curls her tresses to her shoulders flowing?
Honey on the girl and a fine rose on her cheeks,
And every idle fellow thinking she's his own.

Have you seen my gleaming one down beside the wave,
Gold rings on her fingers and she braiding her hair?
This is what Captain Power of the ship did declare,
That he'd rather have herself than all Ireland for his share.

40. Dear Dark Head

A version of this song is also found in Scots Gaelic.

O dear dark head of mine,
   Put your smooth bright arm around me,
O mouth of honey with the taste of thyme,
   Heartless the one that would not give you love!

There are girls in this village distracted and grieved,
   Unloosing their hair to blow free in the wind,
For my sake, the heartiest lad in the land,
   But all of them I would forsake for the darling of my heart.

O dear dark head of mine,
   Put your smooth bright arm around me,
O mouth of honey with the taste of thyme,
   Heartless the one that would not give you love!

41. Cúnla

Agus cé hé sin thíos 'tá a' leagadh na gclathacha?
Cé hé sin thíos 'tá a' leagadh na gclathacha?
Cé hé sin thíos 'tá a' leagadh na gclathacha?
– Mise fhéin, adúirt Cúnla.

'Chúnla, 'chroí, ná teara níos goire dhom,
'Chúnla, 'chroí, ná teara níos goire dhom,
'Chúnla, 'chroí, ná teara níos goire dhom.
– 'Cúis dom sin? arsa Cúnla.

Is cé hé sin thíos 'tá a' bualadh na fuinneoige?
Cé hé sin thíos 'tá a' bualadh na fuinneoige?
Cé hé sin thíos 'tá a' bualadh na fuinneoige?
– Mise fhéin, adúirt Cúnla.

Cé hé sin thíos 'tá a' fadú na tine dhom?
Cé hé sin thíos 'tá a' fadú na tine dhom?
Cé hé sin thíos 'tá a' fadú na tine dhom?
– Mise fhéin, adúirt Cúnla.

Cé hé sin thíos 'tá a' tarrac na pluide dhíom?
Cé hé sin thíos 'tá a' tarrac na pluide dhíom?
Cé hé sin thíos 'tá a' tarrac na pluide dhíom?
– Mise fhéin, adúirt Cúnla.

41. Cúnla

Cúnla *is the local form of the man's name* Connla, *as in No. 3. I print this lively and humorous song in the Connemara version sung by Seosamh Ó hÉanaí. What gives the song its special piquancy is the girl's pretence, as her lover approaches ever nearer, that she does not know who he is and that she does not desire his embraces.*

Who's that below that's knocking the ditches down?
Who's that below that's knocking the ditches down?
Who's that below that's knocking the ditches down?
　　– I myself, said Cúnla.

　　　　Cúnla, darling, come no nearer me.
　　　　Cúnla, darling, come no nearer me.
　　　　Cúnla, darling, come no nearer me.
　　　　　– Why so, now? said Cúnla.

Who's that below that's striking the window?
Who's that below that's striking the window?
Who's that below that's striking the window?
　　– I myself, said Cúnla.

Who's that below that's kindling the fire for me?
Who's that below that's kindling the fire for me?
Who's that below that's kindling the fire for me?
– I myself, said Cúnla.

Who's that below that's pulling the quilt off me?
Who's that below that's pulling the quilt off me?
Who's that below that's pulling the quilt off me?
　　– I myself, said Cúnla.

42. Caoineadh Airt Uí Laoghaire

I

Eibhlín Dhubh: Mo ghrá go daingean tu!
Lá dá bhfaca thu
Ag ceann tí an mhargaidh,
Thug mo shúil aire dhuit,
Thug mo chroí taitneamh duit,
D'éalaíos óm charaid leat
I bhfad ó bhaile leat.

Is domhsa nárbh aithreach:
Chuiris parlús á ghealadh dhom
Rúmanna á mbreacadh dhom,
Bácús á dheargadh dhom,
Brící á gceapadh dhom,
Rósta ar bhearaibh dom,
Mairt á leagadh dhom;
Codladh i gclúmh lachan dom
Go dtíodh an t-eadartha
Nó thairis dá dtaitneadh liom.

42. Lament for Art O Leary

Art O Leary was born about 1747 near Macroom in Co. Cork. While still in his teens he went soldiering to Europe and returned about 1767 with the rank of captain. At this time a young widow from Iveragh in Kerry, Eibhlín Dhubh Ní Conaill, aunt of Daniel O'Connell, saw him on the street of Macroom and fell in love with him, as she describes in our poem. The two got married and set up house at Raleigh (Ráth Laoich) near Macroom. Art became embroiled with a neighbouring Protestant landowner, Abraham Morris, who was high sheriff of Cork and he was killed in an encounter with Morris's men in 1773.

The Lament, *in its two representative basic versions (A, A¹),[1] has the following structure:*

Part I: The main lament by Eibhlín at the scene of his death is largely lyric biography.

Part II, composed in the following days at her home: Words of contention between Eibhlín and Art's sister chiefly. I have not included lines attributed to Art's father.

Part III: Eibhlín continues her Lament. *The vital part of this is included.*

Part IV: Most of this, attributed to Art's sister, is less impressive. I have given only the final stanza, which is attributed to Eibhlín.

Part V, composed after the burial. I include its final sections where Eibhlín concentrates on pure lament.

I

Eibhlín Dhubh: I love you steadfastly!
The day I spied you first,
At the gable-end of the market-house,
My eye observed you well,
My heart warmed to you,
I stole away from my dear one with you,
And went far away with you.

I had no regrets.
You put a parlour whitening for me,
Rooms a-brightening,
An oven reddening,
Brick-loaves a-baking,
Roast meat on spits for me,
Beeves a-slaughtering,
Sleep on eiderdown
Until the milking-hour,
Or later, if I wished.

Mo chara go daingean tu!
Is cuimhin lem aigne
An lá breá earraigh úd,
Gur bhreá thíodh hata dhuit
Faoi bhanda óir tarraingthe,
Claíomh cinn airgid –
Lámh dheas chalma –
Rompsáil bhagarthach –
Fír-chritheagla
Ar námhaid chealgach –
Tú i gcóir chun falaracht,
Is each caol ceannann fút.
D'umhlaídís Sasanaigh síos go talamh duit,
Is ní ar mhaithe leat
Ach le haon-chorp eagla,
Cé gur leo a cailleadh tu,
A mhuirnín mh'anama.

Mo chara thu go daingean!
Is nuair thiocfaidh chugham abhaile
Conchubhar beag an cheana
Is Fear Ó Laoghaire, an leanbh,
Fiafróid díom go tapaidh
Cár fhágas féin a n-athair.
'Neosad dóibh faoi mhairg
Gur fhágas i gCill na Martar.
Glaofaid siad ar a n-athair,
Is ní bheidh sé acu le freagairt.

Mo chara thu go daingean!
Is níor chreideas riamh dod mharbh
Gur tháinig chugham do chapall
Is a srianta léi go talamh,
Is fuil do chroí ar a leacain
Siar go t'iallait ghreanta
Mar a mbítheá id shuí 's id sheasamh.

Thugas léim go tairsigh,
An dara léim go geata,
An tríú léim ar do chapall.
Do bhuaileas go luath mo bhasa
Is do bhaineas as na reathaibh

My own beloved one!
My heart remembers now
That fine Spring afternoon,
How well it suited you:
A hat with golden band,
A sword with silver hilt,
A spirited right hand,
The prance of cavalry
Inspiring mortal fear
In a treacherous enemy;
You were prepared for ambling
On your slender, white-faced horse.
The English used bow to earth to you,
Not for your own good,
But for very dread,
Though 'twas by them you fell,
My soul, my dearest one!

My own beloved one!
And when they come home to me,
Little Connor the affectionate,
The baby, Faar O Leary,
They will quickly ask
Where I left their father,
I will say, in my misery,
I left him in Kilnamartery;
They will call upon their father
And he will not be there to answer.

My own beloved one!
I would not believe you died,
Till your horse came up beside me
With reins to earth sliding,
Your heart's blood on its side-face
And from there to the polished saddle,
Where you would sit or stand upright.

I gave one leap to the threshold,
A second to the gateway,
The third leap to the saddle.
I quickly clapped my hands
And made off at high speed,

Chomh maith is bhí sé agam,
Go bhfuaras romham tu marbh
Cois toirín ísil aitinn,
Gan Pápa gan easpag,
Gan cléireach gan sagart
Do léifeadh ort an tsailm,
Ach seanbhean chríonna chaite
Do leath ort binn dá fallaing –
Do chuid fola leat 'na sraithibh;
Is níor fhanas le hí ghlanadh
Ach í ól suas lem basaibh.

Mo ghrá thu go daingean!
Is éirigh suas id sheasamh
Is tar liom féin abhaile,
Go gcuirfeam mairt á leagadh,
Go nglaofam ar chóisir fhairsing,
Go mbeidh againn ceol á spreagadh,
Go gcóireod duitse leaba
Faoi bhairlíní geala,
Faoi chuilteanna breátha breaca,
A bhainfidh asat allas
In ionad an fhuachta a ghlacais.

II

Deirfiúr Airt: Mo chara is mo stór tu!
Is mó bean chumtha chórach
Ó Chorcaigh na seolta
Go Droichead na Tóime,
Do thabharfadh macha mór bó dhuit
Agus dorn buí-óir duit,
Ná raghadh a chodladh 'na seomra
Oíche do thórraimh.

Eibhlín Dhubh: Mo chara is m' uan tu!
Is ná creid sin uathu,
Ná an cogar a fuarais,
Ná an scéal fir fuatha,
Gur a chodladh a chuas-sa.
Níor throm suan dom:
Ach bhí do linbh ró-bhuartha,

150

As well as I was able,
Till at a stunted furze bush
I found you dead before me,
Without pope or bishop,
Without priest or cleric
To read a psalm over you,
Only an old withered crone
That spread the skirt of her cloak on you;
Your blood was pouring to the ground,
I did not wait to cleanse it,
But with my hands I drank it up.

My love for evermore!
And rise up as before,
And come with me homewards.
We'll slaughter fattened cattle,
Invite many to the party,
We'll have music playing,
And then I'll dress your bed for you
With sheets all snow-white
And fine speckled coverings
That will bring out the sweat
In place of the cold you caught.

II

Art's sister: You are my heart's darling!
And many a fine shapely lady
From Cork of the sails
To the bridge of the Toom
Who would give you a large herd of cows
And a handful of yellow gold,
And would not sleep in her own room
The night of your wake.

Eibhlín Dhubh: My love, my dear one!
Do not believe them,
Nor the hint you got,
Nor the hostile story
That I went to sleep.
Sleep did not come to me,
Your children were sore grieving,

'S do theastaigh sé uathu
Iad a chur chun suaimhnis.

A dhaoine na n-ae istigh,
'Bhfuil aon bhean in Éirinn,
Ó luí na gréine,
A shínfeadh a taobh leis,
Do bhéarfadh trí lao dho,
Ná raghadh le craobhacha
I ndiaidh Airt Uí Laoghaire
Atá anso traochta
Ó mhaidin inné agam?

M'fhada-chreach léan-ghoirt
Ná rabhas-sa taobh leat
Nuair lámhadh an piléar leat,
Go ngeobhainn é im thaobh dheas
Nó i mbinn mo léine,
Is go léigfinn cead slé' leat
A mharcaigh na ré-ghlac.

Deirfiúr Airt: Mo chreach ghéarchúiseach
Ná rabhas ar do chúlaibh
Nuair lámhadh an púdar,
Go ngeobhainn é im chom dheas
Nó i mbinn mo ghúna,
Is go léigfinn cead siúil leat
A mharcaigh na súl nglas,
Ós tú b'fhearr léigean chucu.

III

Eibhlín Dhubh: Mo chara thu is mo shearc-mhaoin!
Is gránna an chóir a chur ar ghaiscíoch
Comhra agus caipín,
Ar mharcach an dea-chroí
A bhíodh ag iascaireacht ar ghlaisíbh
Agus ag ól ar hallaíbh
I bhfarradh mná na ngeal-chíoch.
Mo mhíle mearaí
Mar a chailleas do thaithí.
Greadadh chughat is díth

152

And they needed
To be put at ease then.

O friends of my inmost heart,
Is there a woman in Ireland
Would lie beside him
From set of sun,
Would bear his three babes
And not go raving
For Art O Leary,
Who lies there lifeless
Since early yesterday?

My heartfelt sorrow
I wasn't beside you
When the shot was fired at you,
To take it in my right side,
Or in the skirt of my tunic
And leave you ranging over moorland,
Nimble-handed rider!

Art's sister: My bitter grief
I wasn't behind you
When the powder was ignited,
To take it in my right side,
Or in the fringe of my kirtle,
And leave you free to move,
O grey-eyed rider,
Since 'twas you could best deal with them!

III

Eibhlín Dhubh: My darling, my dearest!
A horrid harness for a champion
Casque and coffin
On the true-hearted horseman,
Who used to fish in burns,
And drink in the wine-halls
With white-bosomed women.
Alas, and alas,
How I have lost your company!
Affliction and death to you,

A Mhorris ghránna an fhill!
A bhain díom fear mo thí
Athair mo leanbh gan aois:
Dís acu ag siúl an tí,
'S an tríú duine acu istigh im chlí,
Agus is dócha ná cuirfead díom.

Mo chara thu is mo thaitneamh!
Nuair ghabhais amach an geata
D'fhillis ar ais go tapaidh,
Do phógais do dhís leanbh,
Do phógais mise ar bharra baise.
Dúraís, 'A Eibhlín, éirigh id sheasamh
Agus cuir do ghnó chun taisce
Go luaimneach is go tapaidh.
Táimse ag fágáil an bhaile,
Is ní móide go deo go gcasfainn.'
Níor dheineas dá chaint ach magadh,
Mar bhíodh á rá liom go minic cheana.

Mo chara thu is mo chuid!
A mharcaigh an chlaímh ghil,
Éirigh suas anois,
Cuir ort do chulaith
Éadaigh uasail ghlain,
Cuir ort do bhéabhar dubh,
Tarraing do lámhainní umat.
Siúd í in airde t'fhuip;
Sin í do láir amuigh.
Buail-se an bóthar caol úd soir
Mar a maolóidh romhat na toir,
Mar a gcaolóidh romhat an sruth,
Mar a n-umhlóidh romhat mná is fir,
Má tá a mbéasa féin acu –
'S is baolach liomsa ná fuil anois.

IV

Tá fhios ag Íosa Críost
Ná beidh caidhp ar bhathas mo chinn,
Ná léine chnis lem thaoibh,
Ná bróg ar thrácht mo bhoinn,

Morris, vile and treacherous,
Who deprived me of my husband,
Father of my infants,
Two of them about the house,
The third one in the womb,
That I may never now bring forth!

My love and my delight!
When you went out the gate
You returned in a trice,
Kissed your two children,
Then you kissed me on the fingertips,
Saying 'Eileen, rise up now
And arrange your affairs
Actively and quickly.
I am leaving home
And may never return.'
His words I took merely as a joke,
He had said it many times before.

My darling, my own one!
Horseman of the bright sword,
Rise upon your feet,
Put on your splendid suit
Of bright clean clothes,
Put on your black beaver hat,
Draw on your slender gloves,
Your whip is there aloft,
Your mare is at the doorstep,
Strike east along the narrow road,
Where the trees will stoop before you,
And the stream will droop before you,
And men and women bow,
If now they know their place, at all,
And much I fear they don't.

IV

Christ Jesus sees and knows
I'll have no covering for my head,
Nor shirt to shield my skin,
Nor shoe on my foot-sole,

Ná trioscán ar fuaid mo thí,
Ná srian leis an láir ndoinn,
Ná caithfidh mé le dlí,
'S go raghad anonn thar toinn
Ag comhrá leis an rí,
'S mara gcuirfidh ionam aon tsuim
Go dtiocfad ar ais arís
Go bodach na fola duibhe
A bhain díom féin mo mhaoin.

V

Mo ghrá thu agus mo rún!
Tá do stácaí ar a mbonn,
Tá do bha buí á gcrú;
Is ar mo chroí atá do chumha
Ná leigheasfadh Cúige Mumhan
Ná Gaibhne Oileáin na bhFionn.
Go dtiocfaidh Art Ó Laoghaire chugham
Ní scaipfidh ar mo chumha
Atá i lár mo chroí á bhrú,
Dúnta suas go dlúth
Mar a bheadh glas a bheadh ar thrúnc
'S go raghadh an eochair amú.

Stadaidh anois d'bhur ngol,
A mhná na súl bhfliuch mbog,
Go nglaofaidh Art Ó Laoghaire deoch,
Agus tuilleadh thar cheann na mbocht,
Sula dtéann isteach don scoil –
Ní hag foghlaim léinn ná port,
Ach ag iompar cré agus cloch.

Nor furniture throughout the house,
Nor bridle for the brown mare
That I will not spend at law.
And I'll fare across the wave[2]
Until I meet the king,
And if he will not heed me,
I'll return again
To the black-blooded boor[3]
That stole my property.

V

My darling, my beloved!
Your stacks are standing firm,
Your yellow cows are milking,
My heart is seared with grief
That all Munster cannot ease,
Nor the druid-smiths of Ireland.
Till Art O Leary comes to me
I will find no release
From the anguish in my breast
Where it's being compressed
Like a lock upon a trunk
When you've mislaid the key.

But cease now from your keening,
O women of the weeping eyes,
Till Art O Leary calls a drink
And a measure for the poor,
Before entering the school –
Not to study tune or lore,
But to bear up clay and stone.

---

1. S. Ó Tuama, *Caoineadh Airt Uí Laoghaire*, Dublin 1961, p. 46.
2. Tradition has it that she did go and that two soldiers were convicted of the murder and transported.
3. Abraham Morris was found guilty of murder and apparently died of a wound inflicted by Art's brother before he could leave Cork.

43. Cúirt an Mheán Oíche

I

Bhí a gruaig léi scaoilte síos go slaodach
Is buaireamh suíte fíor 'na féachaint,
Fuinneamh 'na radharc is faghairt 'na súile
Is fiuchadh le dradhain uilc aighnis fúthu;
A caínt á cosc le loscadh cléibhe,
Gan gíog 'na tost, ach tocht á traochadh;

43. The Midnight Court (Brian Merriman) (1749-1805)

Brian Merriman was born at Ennistymon in West Clare, the son of a small farmer who was also a stone mason. When he was a few years old the family moved to Killaneany near Lough Graney in North-East Clare. Here on eight acres of land Brian later set up a school and taught mathematics for some twenty years (c. 1765-1785). It is said that he composed The Midnight Court *here about 1780. He married about 1787 and had two daughters. In 1802-1803 the Merriman family settled in Limerick city where Brian spent his last years teaching.*

The Midnight Court *is a lengthy comic poem of 1026 verses in rhyming couplets. It comprises:*

A. A Prologue in which the poet introduces his Vision.

B. Three dramatic monologues in which the burning issues are debated in a courtroom before a judge by interested parties.

C. An Epilogue in which judgment is pronounced.

The poem opens with a spirited account of Lough Graney, north of Feakle in Clare, beside which the poet spent his childhood years. It is July, and the poet, drowsed by the heat and the drone of insects, stretches out on the luscious grass and is soon asleep. In his vision he witnesses an upheaval of nature, and out of the storm strides a gigantic female figure round the bend of the lake towards him. In her hand she holds the sheriff's wand of office. She admonishes the sleeper to awaken and hasten to the court at Feakle which is being convened by the fairy host of Moy Graney (on the west side of the lake). Its object is to rectify the social and economic ills of the country and particularly to inquire into the decline of the population and the causes of celibacy among the young. Moved by these evils, the fairies had chosen by lot Eeval (Aoibheall) queen of the Craglee[1] shee, or fairy host, to act as convenor and to undertake the task of rectifying anomalies in Thomond[2] law and life. The sleeper is swept away by the sheriff to the court at Feakle. They reach the spacious well-lit hall which is well-attended by women and others, with Eeval already in the Chair. A beautiful young woman stands distraught at the witness table as our version begins (line 153).

Part I. Plight of the Women

a) *Maiden in Distress (153-166)*

Her hair hung loosely down in wreaths,
Her eyes were very deeply troubled,
Her glance was vigorous and fiery
And seething with contentious spite.
Her words were caught in her scorching breast,
She was speechless, in the throes of stress,

159

B'fhuirist a rá gur bás ba rogha léi,
Is tuile gan tlás ag tál go trom léi,   160
'Na seasamh ar lár an chláir 'na saighead
'S í ag greadadh na lámh 's ag fáscadh a ladhar.
An uair go ghoil sí folcaí fíochmhar
Is d'fhuascail osnaí gothaí a caínte
D'imigh a smúid is d'iompaigh snó uirthi,
Thriomaigh sí a gnúis is dúirt mar 'neosad:

'Míle fáilte is gáirdeas cléibh romhat,
A Aoibheall, a fháidhbhean ársa ón Léithchraig,
A shoilse an lae is a ré gan choimse,
A shaibhreas saolta i ngéibheann daoirse,   170
A cheannasach bhuach ó shluaite an aoibhnis,
Dob easnamh crua thú i dTuain 's i dTír Luirc.
Cúis mo cháis, is fáth mo chaointe,
Cúis do chráigh mé, is d'fhág mé cloíte,
Bhain dem threoir mé, is sheoil gan chiall mé,
Is chaith mar cheo mé dóite i bpianta:
Na sluaite imíonn gan chríoch, gan chaomhnadh,
Ar fuaid an tsaoil seo d'fhíorscoith béithe
'Na gcailleacha dubha gan chumhdach céile,
Caite gan chlú, gan chionta claonbhirt.   180
Is aithnid dom féin sa mhéid seo dem shiúlta
Bean agus céad nár mhéin leo a dhiúltadh
– Is mise 'na measc, mo chreach mar táimse! –
D'imigh 'na spaid gan fear gan pháiste.
Mo dhochar, mo dhódh, mo bhrón mar bhíom,
Gan sochar gan seoid gan só gan síth,
Go doilbhir duaibhseach duamhar dítheach,
Gan chodladh gan suan gan suairceas oíche,
Ach maslaithe i mbuairt, gan suaineas sínte,
Ar leabain leamhfhuar dár suathadh ag smaointe!   190

A cháidh na Craige! breathain go bíogach
Mná na Banba in anacra suíte,
Ar nós, má leanaid na fearaibh dá bhfuadar
Ó, mo lagar, ach caithfeamna a bhfuadach!

Your wife wed for life and till death to her cleave.
It's a pointless task for a woman like me
To expound the words of the law in your presence:
O Pearl of Wisdom, you remember the Bible,
Every point you can establish precisely,
The sweet voice eternal, the power of the words,
And the speech of the Lamb who will not deceive us,
God who would not have His mother a maiden,
And the law of every prophet in favour of ladies...

After appealing to the Queen for the unmarried girls (829-842), the speaker returns to the hard realities of life in Munster:

i) Men are Scarce (843-854)

Alas, alas! My thoughts are vain,
Talking of husbands 'mid fire and flame;
'Tis hard for me hope for wedded delight,
And not a man to three women in Munster this night!
Since this straitened land has encountered such need,
Willing men scarce and the case so urgent,
Ireland empty while weeds grow apace,
The young folk all getting bent and grey,
Suffer no one in sadness to be long unwed
And whatever you do, bring a man to my bed!
Tie them early and meekly into the traces,
Then leave them to us to show them their paces!'

Part IV. The Judgement (855-1024)

Eeval's verdict is that all unmarried males over twenty-one years are to be tied to a tree, stripped and whipped with a cord. The women are to devise suitable punishment for the old bachelors who did not take their marriage chances. Old, impotent men are excused in return for the services they can render by housework and by fully accepting their wives' illegitimate offspring. In regard to clerical celibacy, Eeval proposes patience and discretion in the secure expectation that Pope and Council will yet release the clergy to satisfy the women's need. The inveterate old bachelors must be weeded out. Meanwhile, Eeval has business elsewhere in Munster and when she returns the following month, those elderly men who prey on women to maintain a raffish reputation only, will be sought out and confined.

Suddenly the poet has a horrible presentiment and, sure enough, the gigantic

193

44. Má's Buairt Rómhór

Dhá chailín ó Bhaile na bPoc i bParóiste Múrach, a bhí ag obair síos amach chun Tiobrad Árann, is do thuit duine acu chun drochshláinte. Do labhair a driofúr léi mar leanas. Bhí sí d'iarraidh misneach a thabhairt di chun siubhail abhaile léi:

Má's buairt ró-mhór do luigh ar t'aigne,
Croith dhíot suas í is téanam abhaile liom,
Mar a bhfeicfeam an fhaoileann cois taoide ag screadaigh ann,
Agus radharc bhreágh áluinn ar Ard na Caithne 'gainn.

Taobh Bhaile Dháith ba bhreágh liom amharc air,
Is an Tower go hárd anáirde ar bharra chnuic,
Mar a bhfeicfeam an t-Oileán is an Sceilg Bheannuithe,
Mar a mbíodh Mícheál naomhtha ag léigheamh an Aifrinn.

194

female bailiff pounces upon him and drags him up to the table. She invites the women to survey his body, which though unshapely, is adequate for procreation. Whereupon, she urges them to seize him and begin whipping him unmercifully, so that his cries may terrify the hardened old bachelors of Ireland. And as Eeval signs and dates the Act, the poet, beside himself, awakens from his harrowing vision.

1. Near Killaloe, County Clare.
2. North Munster.
3. I.e. the fairies.
4. Verses 213–4, with their list of adjectives, are omitted here.
5. The reference is to cup-tossing in fortune-telling.
6. Superstitions.
7. One ingredient was from the menses.
8. Food based on milk.
9. Anglo-Irish *greesa*, Irish *gríosach* 'ashes'. He threatened to place the baby on the hot ashes to determine if it was a fairy changeling or a human baby. The *greesa* would rout a changeling.
10. The horns which were supposed to grow on the cuckold's head.
11. One of the Fianna.
12. Literally, Acheron, a river in Hades over which the souls of the dead were ferried.
13. The reference is to clerical celibacy, as in line 587 *cuing na cléire* 'the yoke of the clerics'. *Cumha* can mean 1) condition or arrangement; 2) pining; sexual desire. A *double entendre* is likely here.

44. If 'Twas Too Great a Sadness

Two girls from Baile na bPoc in the parish of Moor[1] were working down the country, Tipperary way, and one of them fell into bad health. Her sister spoke to her as follows – she was trying to encourage her to walk home with her:

If 'twas too great a sadness that preyed on your mind,
Shake it right off you and come back home with me,
Where we'll see the seagull cry by the tide
And the beautiful prospect of Ard na Caithne.[2]

The side of Baile Dháith[3] I'd love to see before me
And the Tower above it rising high on the hill,
There we can view the Island[4] and holy Skellig[5]
Where Mass used be said by the blessed Michael.

195

Mo ghrádh-sa Duibhneach', 'sí dob fhearra liom,
Agus Carraig an Fhíona taoibh le Galarus,
Baile na nGall mar a mbíonn greann ag fearaibh ann,
Ar a' gcnocán muar atá ar bhruach na fairrge.

45. Gein Nár Milleadh (Eibhlín Ní Mhurchú)

Níor chreid mo chroí go dtiocfadh lá
Ná beadh sé romham ar dhul abhaile dhom,
Ach tháinig lá a thug tuairisc báis
An té dob' athair dom.
Bhí an t-aos ann, cheithre fichid bliain
Agus dosaon fairis sin.
Is é adubhairt sé fhéin
Go raibh marc ar sheal gach n-aon ar a theacht,
Ach go gcaithfí fanacht
Go sroichfí an marc,
Is ansan, gan aon dá rogha, imeacht.

I ndeireadh a shaoil ní raibh sé bodhar;
Ní raibh, ná dall;
Ach bhí focail ann nár thuig.
Oíche cois tine dúinn beirt
Chuir sé chugam a' cheist:
'An *pill* seo atá faoi chaibidil,
Cad é fhéinig, abair liom.'

Do stad mo chroí,
D'fhuar is d'fháisc,

Duibhneach's[6] my darling, she's my favourite,
With Carriganeena, near to Gallarus,
Baile na nGall where men find diversion
On the spacious headland beside the sea.

1. Known also as Kilquane parish, lying north-east of Smerwick Harbour, west Kerry.
2. Smerwick.
3. Ballydavid.
4. Blasket Island.
5. In Irish also Sceilg Mhichíl 'Skellig of Saint Michael', Michael being patron of high places and this famous monastic site a lofty rock off the Iveragh Peninsula to the south.
6. Corca Dhuibhne 'Corkaguiny', the Dingle Peninsula. The other three places mentioned in this stanza lie on the southern and south-eastern coast of Smerwick Harbour.

45. The Unaborted

My heart never thought the day would come
He would not be there when I got home,
But a day came that brought death tidings
Of the one that fathered me.
He was old: four score years
And twelve to boot.
As he himself said:
Each one's span was marked at birth
And one had to wait
Till the mark was reached,
And then, like it or not, depart.

At the end of his days he was not deaf;
Nor was he blind;
But words there were he did not understand.
One night, as we two sat by the fire,
He put me the question:
'This *pill* they are talking about,
Tell me now, what is it?'

My heart went still,
Chilled, clutched tight,

197

Bhíos i dteannta, ní raibh dul as agam,
Bhí ceist chruaidh im' láthair,
Is é siúd ag súil le freagra.
Chuimhníos ar mo chlann fhéin,
Is mé ag réiteach a gcuid ceisteanna,
Ag míniú cúrsaí an tsaoil dóibh,
Is go deimhin, do fuaireas deacair é;
'An fhírinne ghlan a insint'
A chomhairligh lucht na h-eagna –
Gan seoid a' bharra a cheilt orthu,
Nó gur dóibh siúd ba mheasaide é.

Ach ceist a theacht óm' athair chugam!
B'shin rud nár gheal orm
Go dtitfeadh sé mar chrann orm
An *pill* a léamh do sheanduine
A chonaic sliocht ar shliocht a shleachta fhéin;
Fear nár mhothaigh riamh aon doicheall
Roimh aon abhras breise clainne
A chuir sé fhéin mar mhuirear
Ar shaothar a chuid allais
Ar muir agus ar talamh
Gan leas sóisialta ná liúntas leanbh.

Níorbh aon tráth 'scéal thairis' é,
Ná tráth staire seanchais.
Dheineas ar nós na leanbh leis,
Scaoileas chuige an teachtaireacht
Le siollaí gearra seachantach'
Go raibh an *pill* ann
Chun cosc a chur ar chlann
Agus ceann a scaoileadh le colainn.
Níor labhair,
Ní dubhartsa a thuilleadh
Ach féachaint uaim isteach i gcroí na tine.

Ansúd istigh do dhearcas
Mé fhéin in aois a deich
Is mé lánchinnte dearfa
Gur ag baint fheamainne
A bhí sé siúd roimh lá
Nuair a tháinig sé ormsa
Im' bhunóic ar lagtrá.

I was trapped, there was no escape:
A question hard to grapple,
And he there expecting an answer!
I thought of my own children,
And I answering their questions for them,
Explaining to them the world's ways,
And, no mistake, I found it hard;
'Tell the unvarnished truth'
Was the counsel of the wise –
Not a jot at all conceal,
Or they themselves will be the worse of it.

But to be questioned by my father!
That I never expected:
That it should fall to my lot
To explain the *pill* to an old man
Who had seen his seed to the fourth generation,
A man who never felt anything but welcome
Should another child come, though exceeding
The family he thought filled the measure
Of his work by the sweat of his brow
On sea and on land,
Without social welfare or children's allowance.

It was no time for topic-changing
Or for telling ancient tales.
I answered him as I would my children,
I let him have the message
In short and wary words
That the *pill* was there
So as not to have babies
And allow the body its own way.
He did not speak,
I said no more myself
But looked into the heart of the fire.

There within I saw
Myself at the age of ten
And I certain sure and positive
That it was cutting seaweed
He was before daybreak,
When he found me, a newborn babe,
At ebb-tide on the strand.

Chuir sé isteach ar mo phictiúir:
'Mhuise, n'fheadar,' ar seisean go smaointeach,
'B'fhearr scaoileadh leis an nádúir!'

Ó ba thráth ceisteanna é,
Bhí ceist agam do fhéinig:
'An gcreideann tú, ' arsa mise
'Go bhfuil saol eile i ndiaidh an tsaoil seo?'
D'fhreagair sé ná feadair sé
Ach go mb'fhearr leis fhéin bheith réidh do.

Níor chreid mo chroí go dtiocfadh lá
Ná beadh sé romham ar dhul abhaile dhom,
Ach tháinig lá a thug tuairisc báis
An té dob' athair dom.
Anois níl rud ar domhan
Ná tuigeann sé, más fíor
Go bhfuil saol eile ann.

46. Caoineadh (Máire Mhac an tSaoi)

Glór goil ar an ngaoith
Is brat síne liathaigh spéartha,
Ise dob áille fág ina luí
Ina caoluaigh chúng ina haonar.

Tiocfaidh an leoithne bhog aniar
Is an duilliúr úr ar lomaghéaga,
Líonfaidh ré is éireoidh grian,
Ina gcúrsa síor triallfaidh réalta;

Is as an gcré tá os a cionn,
As a hucht geal, as a caomhchorp,
Trí aoibh an lae is deora ón ndrúcht,
Trí fhód aníos fásfaidh féara –

Ach choíche ní cúmfar ceol ceart,
Feasta, ná caoinvéarsa;
Cailleann anois an croí a neart
Is an mheabhair ghlic, cailleann a héifeacht.

He cut across this image:
'Wisha, I don't know,' he said thoughtfully,
'Better let nature take its course!'

As it was question time,
I put to him the question:
'Do you believe,' said I
'In another world after this one?'
He said he didn't know,
But would prefer to be ready for it.

My heart never thought the day would come
He would not be there when I got home,
But a day came that brought death tidings
Of the one that fathered me.
And now there's nothing in the world
He does not know, if it's a thing
That there's another world.

46. Lament

The cry of weeping on the wind
And a rain-mantle greying skies,
She the loveliest one leave lying
Alone in her narrow grave confined.

The soft breeze will come from the west
And foliage fresh on naked branches,
Moon will fill and sun rise
And stars traverse their eternal cycle;

And out of the clay that's over her,
From her bright breast, her body fair,
Through smiling day and drops of dew,
Through the earth will spring up grasses –

But nevermore will true music
Or beauteous verse be composed;
Now the heart its strength loses
And the nimble mind loses its force.

47. Finit (Máire Mhac an tSaoi)

Le seans a chuala uathu scéala an chleamhnais
Is b'ait liom srian le héadroime na gaoithe –
Do bhís chomh hanamúil léi, chomh domheabhartha,
Chomh fiáin léi, is chomh haonraic, mar ba chuimhin liom.

Féach feasta go bhfuil dála cháich i ndán duit,
Cruatan is coitinne, séasúr go céile,
Ag éalú i ndearúd le hiompú ráithe
Gur dabht arbh ann duit riamh, ná dod leithéidse...

Ach go mbeidh poirt anois ná cloisfead choíche
Gan tú bheith os mo chomhair arís sa chúinne
Ag feitheamh, ceol ar láimh leat, roimh an rince
Is diamhaireacht na hoíche amuigh id shúile.

48. Labhrann Deirdre (Máire Mhac an tSaoi)

Ar bhruach na coille
Chonac ag dul tharam
An triúr laoch
Dob áille dealbh,
Is do lean mo chroí-se
An té dob fhearra,
Cé go rabhas-sa snaidhmthe
Le rímhac Neasa.

A Naois' mhic Uisnigh,
A réalt chatha,
Ba bheo do ghrua
Ná an fhuil sa tsneachta,
Mar sciath an fhéich
Bhí do dhlúthfholt daite,
Is ceann Chonchúir
Féna ualach seaca.

I bpálás Eamhna
Tá tinte ar lasadh,
Is grianán scáileach

47. Finit

By chance I heard from them the news your match was made,
And I thought: how strange to curb the lightness of the wind –
As spirited you were, as enigmatic,
As wild, as lonely – the way that I remembered.

See how henceforth your fate will be like others',
Hardship, the common lot, season by season,
Fading to oblivion as each quarter turns,
Until one doubts you ever lived – or any like you.

Except that now there will be tunes I'll hear no more
Without you in the corner here before me,
Waiting, poised to play, before the dancing,
And in your eyes the mystery of the night outside.

48. Deirdre Speaks

At the edge of the wood
I saw going past me
The three warriors
Of loveliest shape,
And my heart followed
The one that was best,
Although I was bound
To the royal son of Ness.[1]

O Niece, son of Ushna,
O star of battle,
Brighter was your cheek
Than blood in the snow;
The hue of the raven's wing
Was on your clustering hair,
And Connor's head weighed down
With its frosty burden.

In the palace of Evin[2]
Fires are lighted
And a sun-bright bower

Romham tá ceaptha,
Is seanóir liath
Ann a d'fhanann
Ná luífead go brách
Len ais mar leannán.

Cá tairbhe domhsa
Staonadh feasta
Ó tá i ndán dom
Ulaidh a chreachadh?
Raghadsa, a ghrá,
Ag éalú leatsa
Sara gcloífead le fear
Is sine ná m'athair.

A bhean sa chúinne,
Éir' it sheasamh
Is gléas orm gúna
Den tsróll dearg;
Le lásaí óir
Beidh mo bhróga ceangailte
Ag siúl lem stór
Thar bhánta an earraigh dom.

49. Táimid Damanta, A Dheirféaracha (Nuala Ní Dhomhnaill)

Táimid damanta, a dheirféaracha,
sinne a chuaigh ag snámh
ar thránna istoíche is na réalta
ag gáirí in aonacht linn,
an mhéarnáil inár dtimpeall
is sinn ag scréachaíl le haoibhneas
is le fionnuaire na taoide,
gan gúnaí orainn ná léinte
ach sinn chomh naíonta le leanaí bliana,
táimid damanta, a dheirféaracha.

Is designed for me,
And waiting there
A grey old man,[1]
By whose side as lover
I'll never lie.

What good for me
Is restraint henceforward,
Since I am fated
To lay waste Ulster?
I will go, my love,
We'll elope together,
Ere I'll live with a man
Older than my father.

O woman in the corner,
Rise and stand now
And array me in a gown
Of scarlet satin;
With golden laces
Will my shoes be fastened,
As I walk with my dearest
Over vernal pastures.

1. King Connor
2. Now Navan Fort, near Armagh.

49. Sisters, We are Damned

Sisters, we are damned,
We who went swimming
On strands by night, with the stars
Laughing in our company,
Phosphorescence all about us
As we screamed with delight
And the freshness of the tide;
Wearing neither dress nor shirt,
As innocent as year-old babes;
Sisters, we are damned.

Táimid damanta, a dheirféaracha,
sinne a thug dúshlán na sagart
is na ngaolta, a d'ith as mias na cinniúna,
a fuair fios oilc is maitheasa
chun gur chuma linn anois mar gheall air.
Chaitheamair oícheanta ar bhántaibh Párthais
ag ithe úll is spíonán is róiseanna
laistiar dár gcluasa, ag rá amhrán
timpeall tinte cnámh na ngadaithe,
ag ól is ag rangás le mairnéalaigh agus robálaithe
is táimid damanta, a dheirféaracha.

Níor chuireamair cliath ar stoca
níor chíoramair, níor shlámamair,
níor thuigeamair de bhanlámhaibh
ach an ceann atá ins na Flaithis in airde.
B'fhearr linn ár mbróga a chaitheamh dínn ar bharra taoide
is rince aonair a dhéanamh ar an ngaineamh fliuch
is port an phíobaire ag teacht aniar chughainn
ar ghaotha fiala an Earraigh, ná bheith fanta
istigh age baile ag déanamh tae láidir d'fhearaibh,
is táimid damanta, a dheirféaracha.

Beidh ár súile ag na péisteanna
is ár mbéala ag na portáin,
is tabharfar fós ár n-aenna
le n-ithe do mhadraí na mbailte fearainn.
Stracfar an ghruaig dár gceannaibh
is bainfear an fheoil dár gcnámha,
geofar síolta úll is craiceann spíonán
i measc rianta ár gcuid urlacan
nuair a bheimid damanta, a dheirféaracha.

Sisters, we are damned,
We who challenged priests
And relatives, who supped from the dish of destiny
And got knowledge of evil and of good,
So that now it does not trouble us.
Nights we spent on fields of paradise
Eating apples and gooseberries, with roses
Behind our ears, singing
Around thieves' bonfires,
Drinking and frolicking with sailors and robbers
And, sisters, we are damned.

We did not darn a stocking,
We neither combed nor carded,
Of *bandles*¹ we only knew
What can be seen in the heavens.
We preferred to take off our shoes at high tide
And dance solo in the wet sand
With the piper's tune coming east to us
On the bountiful winds of Spring, than to bide
At home within, making strong tea for men,
And sisters, we are damned.

The worms will have our eyes
And the crabfish our lips,
Our livers will be thrown
To the dogs of the townlands.
From our heads the hair will be torn
And the flesh from our bones.
Apple seeds and gooseberry skins
Will be found in the traces of our vomit,
Sisters, when we are damned.

1. Ir. *Banlámh*, Anglo-Irish *bandle:* 1) a measure for cloth, of 21 inches; 2) (*astron.*) Orion's belt.

50. Féar Suaithinseach (Nuala Ní Dhomhnaill)
Fianaise an chailín i ngreim 'Anorexia'

Nuair a bhís i do shagart naofa
i lár an Aifrinn, faoi do róbaí corcra
t'fhallaing lín, do stól, do chasal,
do chonnaicís m'aghaidh-se ins an slua
a bhí ag teacht chun comaoineach chughat
is thit uait an abhlainn bheannaithe.

Mise, ní dúrt aon ní ina thaobh.
Bhí náire orm.
Bhí glas ar mo bhéal.
Ach fós do luigh sé ar mo chroí
mar dhealg láibe, gur dhein sé slí
dó fhéin istigh im ae is im lár
gur dhóbair go bhfaighinn bás dá bharr.

Ní fada nó gur thiteas 'on leabaidh;
oideasaí leighis do triaileadh ina gcéadtaibh,
do tháinig chugham dochtúirí, sagairt is bráithre
is n'fhéadadar mé a thabhairt chun sláinte
ach thugadar suas i seilbh bháis me.

Is téigí amach, a fheara,
tugaíg libh rámhainn is speala
corráin, grafáin is sluaiste.
Réabaíg an seanafhothrach,
bearraíg na sceacha, glanaíg an luifearnach,
an slámas fáis, an brus, an ainnise
a fhás ar thalamh bán mo thubaiste.

Is ins an ionad inar thit
an chomaoine naofa féach go mbeidh
i lár an bhiorlamais istigh
toirtín d'fhéar suaithinseach.

Tagadh an sagart is lena mhéireanna
beireadh sé go haiclí ar an gcomaoine naofa
is tugtar chugham í, ar mo theanga
leáfaidh sí, is éireod aniar sa leaba
chomh slán folláin is a bhíos is mé i mo leanbh.

50. Special Grass

The evidence of a girl suffering from Anorexia

When you were a holy priest
In the middle of Mass in your purple robes,
Your linen surplice, your stole, your chasuble,
You saw my face in the crowd
Coming towards you for Communion
And the Consecrated Host fell from your fingers.

As for me, I never mentioned it;
I was ashamed,
My lips were sealed.
And yet it pressed upon my heart
Like a thorn in the mud, until it pierced
To my heart's core,
So that I nearly died of it.

Soon I had to take to my bed;
Doctors' prescriptions were tried by the hundred,
Physicians came to me, priests and friars,
And they failed to restore me to health,
But instead gave me over to death.

And now, men, let ye go out,
Bring spades and scythes,
Sickles, hoes and shovels,
Dig up the old ruin,
Cut back the bushes, clear out the weeds,
The undergrowth, the bits and pieces, the squalid mess
Which grew on the lea-land of my mischance.

And note well that in the place
The Consecrated Host fell there will be
A little tuft of *special grass*
In the middle of the weeds inside.

Let the priest come and with his fingers
Nimbly take the Host
And bring it to me; on my tongue
It will melt and I'll rise up in the bed
As hale and hearty as I was when a child.

51. A Chroí Tincéara (Nuala Ní Dhomhnaill)

Is ná raghfá chun suain anois ar deireadh,
a chroí tincéara,
ná ligfeá suas don ruaille buaille,
don ghliotram is gleo ard i gcónaí,
do bheith ag rúideadh eascainí ó thaobh sráide lá aonaigh,
do bheith ag bualadh buillí marfacha le do chrobh hucstaera,
rian na draoibe i do ríobal is tú ag gabháil cosnochta
murc marc thar nósanna an phobail,
scun scan as radharc na ndaoine,
tré mhóinte is tré churraithe
is gan aon bheann agat ar éinne,
is ná raghfá chun suain anois, a chroí tincéara.

Tánn tú chomh guagach le báidín mearathail,
chomh fiain le giorria a léimfeadh gach súilín ribe
a choimeádann coinín, chomh teasaí leis an láirín bhuí
nár shuigh aon mharcach riamh ar a muin,
chomh righin le gad sailí,
chomh héaganta le muc bhaineann,
is go bhfóire Dia orm má chaithim bheith de shíor
ag glanadh suas an tranglaim a fhágann tú i do dhiaidh; –
an cheirt leata ar gach tor,
an fear ar adhastar ins gach baile fearainn.

Ná tuigeann tú go gcaitheann tú iasc a bheiriú
sula slogann tú siar é,
gan a bheith ag rince Caidhp an Chúil Aird
ar bharaillí pórtair.
Cuimhnigh gur chóir suí chun do mhún a ligint.
Ardaigh beann do ghúnaí aníos ón bpluda.
Cíor do mhothal gruaige.
Tairrig do sheál i gceart aníos thar do ghuaille
mar a dhéanfadh bean mhaith
is ná lig síos mé a thuilleadh,
a ghadsádaí diabhail!, a chroí, a chladhaire.

Caith uait an laochas is díol an mangarae
a iompraíonn tú thart ó bhaile go baile.
Croith tú féin suas is cuir sálaí

51. O Heart of a Tinker

And would you not go to sleep at long last now,
Heart of a tinker!
Would you not cease your wild commotion,
Your hubbub and eternal loud din,
Hurling curses from street pavements on fair-days,
Striking deadly blows with your huckster's paw,
Mud-spattered, bedraggled, while you tramp
Bare-footed, heedless, over the customs of the people
And out of their sight completely,
Through bogs and marshes,
Caring for no one;
And would you not go to sleep now, heart of a tinker!

You are as fickle as a little whirlboat,
As wild as a hare that would jump
Over every rabbit snare, as fiery as the little yellow mare
That never had a rider on her back,
As tough as a willow withe,
As giddy as a female pig,
And God help me if I always must
Be cleaning up the mess you leave behind you,
The rag spread on every bush,
The man on a halter in each townland.

Don't you know you must boil a fish
Before you swallow it,
And not be dancing High-Caul Cap
On porter barrels.
Remember you should sit down to make your pee.
Raise the peak of your dresses from the mire.
Comb your bushy head of hair.
Draw your shawl properly over your shoulder
Like a good woman
And don't let me down any more,
You devil's imp, you darling, you rogue!

Give up the bravado and sell the junk
You carry around from town to town.
Shake yourself up and put high heels

arda faoi do bhróga is búclaí córacha.
Bíodh cleite i do chaipín, is airgead i do sparán,
bain díom aghaidh do chaoraíochta, maith an cailín!
Is ní fada anois
go mbeir teanntaithe agam i gceart,
is ceangal na gcúig gcaol ort,
is dar Rí na bhFeart! mura n-iompaíonn tú timpeall
is cloí leis an gceart
bíodh an diabhal agat sa deireadh, a chroí tincéara.

On your shoes and shapely buckles.
Put a feather in your cap, and money in your purse;
Spare me your abuse – good girl!
And soon now
I'll have you hemmed in properly
And bound hand and foot;
And by the Almighty! Unless you turn round
And stay on the right track,
You can go to the devil in the end, heart of a tinker!

Abbreviations

AGCC	D. Hyde, *Abhráin Ghrádha Chúige Chonnacht,* Dublin, 1905.
Anecd.	*Anecdota from Irish Manuscripts,* ed. Bergin, Best, Meyer, O'Keeffe, Dublin, 1907-13.
Corp. Gen.	*Corpus Genealogiarum Hiberniae,* ed. O'Brien, 1962.
DG	T. F. O'Rahilly, *Dánta Grádha,* Dublin, 1926.
DuG	R. Ní Ógáin, *Duanaire Gaedhilge* I, Dublin, 1921.
EIL	G. Murphy, *Early Irish Lyrics,* Oxford, 1956.
GTIP	D. Greene, F. O'Connor, *A Golden Treasury of Irish Poetry,* London, 1967.
IT	*Irische Texte,* ed. W. Stokes, E. Windisch, Leipzig, 1880-1909.
LL	*Book of Leinster,* ed. Best, Bergin, O'Brien, Dublin, 1954-67.
LU	*Lebor na hUidre,* ed. R. I. Best, O. Bergin, Dublin, 1929.
MIP	T. F. O'Rahilly, *A Miscellany of Irish Proverbs,* Dublin, 1922.
Misc. Hib.	K. Meyer, *Miscellanea Hibernica,* Illinois, 1916.
ND	*Nua-Dhuanaire I-III,* ed. P. de Brún, B. Ó Buachalla, T. Ó Concheanainn, Dublin, 1971-78.
PRIA	*Proceedings of the Royal Irish Academy.*
RIA	Royal Irish Academy.
SI	D. O'Sullivan, *Songs of the Irish,* Dublin, 1960.
SM	An Seabhac, *Seanfhocail na Muimhneach,* Dublin, 1926.
ZCP	Zeitschrift für celtische Philologie.

Bibliographical

1. LL 259 b; V. Hull, *Longes mac n-Uislenn*, New York, 1949.
2. LU p. 122-3; M. Dillon, ed. *Serglige Con Culainn*, Dublin, 1953; GTIP p. 130.
3. LU p. 302 ff.; ZCP 17 p. 193 ff.; *Etudes Celtiques* 14, p. 207 ff.
4. IT III p. 53; K. Meyer, *Miscellanea Hibernica* p. 19, Illinois, 1917; GTIP p. 33.
5. EIL p. 74 ff.; GTIP p. 48 ff.
6. LL 49 b; K. Meyer, *Anecdota from Irish Manuscripts* I, Dublin, 1907, p. 7 ff., GTIP p. 67 ff.
7. IT III p. 71; K. Meyer, *Miscellanea Hibernica* p. 45.
8. K. Meyer, ed. *Liadain and Cuirithir*, London, 1902; EIL p. 82 ff.; GTIP p. 72 ff.
9. LL 278 a; K. Meyer, ed. *Ériu* I 67; EIL p. 6 ff.
10. LL 272 b; D. Greene, ed. *Fingal Rónáin*, Dublin, 1955; GTIP p. 93 ff.
11. K. Meyer, *Fianaigecht* p. 1 ff., Dublin, 1910; GTIP p. 86 ff.
12. K. Meyer ed. *Ériu* II 15; EIL p. 86 ff.; GTIP p. 78 ff.
13. K. Meyer, ed. *Tecosca Cormaic*, RIA Todd Lecture Series 15, Dublin, 1909.
14. K. Meyer, RIA Todd Lecture Series 13, Dublin, 1906.
15. K. Meyer, ed. *Ériu* III 148; EIL p. 50.
16. K. Meyer, ed. *Gaelic Journal* IV p. 88; GTIP p. 191 ff.
17. DG p. 133; ND I p. 15.
18. DG p. 132.
19. DG p. 25.
20. DG p. 34.
21. SM; MIP.
22. SM; oral sources.
23. T. S. Ó Máille, *Seanfhocla Chonnacht* I, II, Dublin, 1948-52.
24. É. ua Muirgheasa, *Seanfhocla Ulad*, Dublin, 1907, 1931.
25. ND I p. 88.
26. S. Ó Duibhginn, *Dónall Óg*, Dublin, 1960; DuG p. 46 ff.
27. ND I p. 82.
28. SI p. 54.
29. SI p. 56.
30. B.Ó Conaire, *Éigse* p. 193, Dublin, 1974.
31. AGCC p. 92 ff.; SI p. 47.

32. AGCC p. 8 ff.; ND III pp. 44-5, 95.
33. SI p. 75 f.
34. SI p. 68 ff.
35. SI p. 58 ff.
36. Ceirnín Ghael Linn CEF 028.
37. AGCC p. 28 ff.; ND III p. 30.
38. DuG p. 69 f.
39. DuG p. 29.
40. ND III pp. 62-3.
41. Ceirnín Ghael Linn CEF 028.
42. S. Ó Tuama ed. *Caoineadh Airt Uí Laoghaire*, Dublin, 1961.
43. D. Ó hUaithne, S. Ó Tuama ed. *Cúirt an Mheán Oíche*, Dublin, 1968.
44. S. Ó Dubhda, *Duanaire Duibhneach* p. 105, Dublin, 1933.
45. E. Ní Mhurchú's manuscript.
46-48. Máire Mhac an tSaoi, *An Cion go dtí Seo*, Dublin, 1987.
49-51. Nuala Ní Dhomhnaill, *Féar Suaithinseach*, Maynooth, 1984.

Acknowledgments

The author and publishers wish to thank all those who have kindly given them permission to make use of copyright material. They are:

Oxford University Press, for permission to use G. Murphy's *Early Irish Lyrics* (1956), Poems 7, 21, 34, 35, 36; The Educational Co. of Ireland for permission to use R. Ní Ógáin's *Duanaire Gaedhilge* I (1921), Poems 21, 40, 58, and a number of proverbs from an Seabhac's *Seanfhocail na Muimhneach* (1926); The Douglas Hyde Trust for Poems 31, 37; the Royal Irish Academy for the use of *Lebor na hUidre* (1929) and of K. Meyer's editions of *The Triads of Ireland* (1906) and the *Instructions of King Cormac* (1909).

Táim faoi chomaoin ag Cumann Merriman, do cheadaigh dom leas a bhaint as *Cúirt an Mheán Oíche* in eagar ag D. Ó hUaithne agus S. Ó Tuama (1968); Scoil an Léinn Cheiltigh, Institiúid Ard-Léinn Bhaile Átha Cliath as na heagráin seo leanas: Serglige *Con Culainn* (1953), *Fingal Rónáin* (1955), *Nua-Dhuanaire* I (1971) Uimhreacha 58, 64 agus *Nua-Dhuanaire* III (1978), Uimhreacha 23, 43, 61; Conradh na Gaeilge, do cheadaigh dom leas a bhaint as *Seanfhocla Uladh* (1907) in eagar ag É. ua Muirgheasa; Gael Linn as focail dhá amhrán le Seosamh Ó hÉanaí ar cheirnín 028; An Sagart, Maigh Nuad as trí dhán le Nuala Ní Dhomhnaill ón duanaire *Féar Suaithinseach* (1984); Sáirséal Ó Marcaigh i ngeall ar thrí dhán le Máire Mhac an tSaoi as *An Cion go dtí Seo* (1987); An Gúm as dán 41, *Duanaire Duibhneach* (1933) in eagar ag S. Ó Dubhda, maraon le dán 96 as an duanaire *Éigse*, in eagar ag B. Ó Conaire, agus fós i ngeall ar líon seanfhocal as *Seanfhocla Chonnacht* (1948-52) in eagar ag T. S. Ó Máille; an Clóchomhar Teoranta as *Caoineadh Airt Uí Laoghaire* (1961) in eagar ag S. Ó Tuama; an t-ollamh Brian Ó Cuív agus Iontaobhas Thomáis F. Í Raithile as *Dánta Grádha* (1926), Uimhreacha 18, 26, 99, 100, agus as cúpla seanfhocal ón *Miscellany of Irish Proverbs* (1922).

The author regrets that in spite of repeated efforts it has proved impossible to contact the holders of copyright in a few cases.